ESSENTIALS OF
Ideal-Type Analysis

Essentials of Qualitative Methods Series

Essentials of Autoethnography
  Christopher N. Poulos

Essentials of Consensual Qualitative Research
  Clara E. Hill and Sarah Knox

Essentials of Critical-Constructivist Grounded Theory Research
  Heidi M. Levitt

Essentials of Descriptive-Interpretive Qualitative Research: A Generic Approach
  Robert Elliott and Ladislav Timulak

Essentials of Discursive Psychology
  Linda M. McMullen

Essentials of Ideal-Type Analysis: A Qualitative Approach to Constructing Typologies
  Emily Stapley, Sally O'Keeffe, and Nick Midgley

ESSENTIALS OF

Ideal-Type Analysis

A Qualitative Approach to Constructing Typologies

Emily Stapley
Sally O'Keeffe
Nick Midgley

 AMERICAN PSYCHOLOGICAL ASSOCIATION

The opinions and statements published are the responsibility of the authors, and such opinions and statements do not necessarily represent the policies of the American Psychological Association.

Published by
American Psychological Association
750 First Street, NE
Washington, DC 20002
https://www.apa.org

Order Department
https://www.apa.org/pubs/books
order@apa.org

In the U.K., Europe, Africa, and the Middle East, copies may be ordered from Eurospan
https://www.eurospanbookstore.com/apa
info@eurospangroup.com

Typeset in Charter and Interstate by Circle Graphics, Inc., Reisterstown, MD

Printer: Gasch Printing, Odenton, MD
Cover Designer: Anne C. Kerns, Anne Likes Red, Inc., Silver Spring, MD

Library of Congress Cataloging-in-Publication Data

Names: Stapley, Emily, author. | O'Keeffe, Sally, author. | Midgley, Nick, author.
Title: Essentials of ideal-type analysis : a qualitative approach to constructing
  typologies / by Emily Stapley, Sally O'Keeffe, and Nick Midgley.
Description: Washington, DC : American Psychological Association, [2021] |
  Series: Essentials of qualitative methods | Includes bibliographical references
  and index.
Identifiers: LCCN 2020045199 (print) | LCCN 2020045200 (ebook) |
  ISBN 9781433834530 (paperback) | ISBN 9781433836909 (ebook)
Subjects: LCSH: Typology (Psychology)—Research—Methodology. |
  Qualitative research—Methodology.
Classification: LCC BF698.3 .S727 2021 (print) | LCC BF698.3 (ebook) |
  DDC 155.2/64—dc23
LC record available at https://lccn.loc.gov/2020045199
LC ebook record available at https://lccn.loc.gov/2020045200

https://doi.org/10.1037/0000235-000

Printed in the United States of America

10 9 8 7 6 5 4 3 2 1

Contents

Series Foreword—Clara E. Hill and Sarah Knox   *vii*

1. Conceptual Foundations   **3**
     Constructing Typologies in Psychology   *4*
     Historical and Epistemological Underpinnings of Ideal-Type Analysis   *5*
     Situating Ideal-Type Analysis Within the Qualitative Research Tradition   *9*
     Key Features of Ideal-Type Analysis   *11*
     Summary   *14*

2. Designing the Study and Collecting the Data   **15**
     What Research Questions Can Ideal-Type Analysis Be Used to Answer?   *15*
     What Size and Type of Sample Are Appropriate for Ideal-Type Analysis?   *17*
     What Data Do I Need to Collect for Ideal-Type Analysis?   *18*
     Do I Need a Research Team to Be Able to Conduct Ideal-Type Analysis?   *21*
     How Do I Manage Researcher Subjectivity in Ideal-Type Analysis?   *23*
     Summary   *25*

3. Analyzing the Data   **27**
     Step 1: Becoming Familiarized With the Data Set   *29*
     Step 2: Writing the Case Reconstructions   *29*
     Step 3: Constructing the Ideal Types   *34*
     Step 4: Identifying the Optimal Cases   *39*
     Step 5: Forming the Ideal-Type Descriptions   *41*
     Step 6: Checking Credibility   *43*
     Step 7: Making Comparisons   *45*
     Summary   *47*

4. Writing the Manuscript   **49**

Writing the Introduction   49

Writing the Methodology Section   50

Writing the Results Section   51

Writing the Discussion Section   53

Summary   53

5. Variations on the Method   **55**

Ideal-Type Analysis With Longitudinal Qualitative Data   56

Ideal-Type Analysis With Qualitative Data From Multiple Groups of
Participants   57

Ideal-Type Analysis With Multiple Types of Data   57

Ideal-Type Analysis as the Second Stage of Qualitative Data Analysis   58

Summary   59

6. An Example of an Ideal-Type Analysis—From Start to Finish   **61**

Developing My Research Question   61

Context for This Study   62

The Sample   63

Data Collection   63

Ethical Considerations   64

Deciding How to Analyze the Data   65

Defining My Epistemological Position   66

Analyzing the Data   67

Writing the Manuscript   77

Summary   78

7. Summary and Conclusions   **79**

Benefits and Advantages of the Method   80

Limitations of the Method   80

Conclusions   82

References   83

Index   93

About the Authors   97

About the Series Editors   99

Series Foreword

Qualitative approaches have become accepted and indeed embraced as empirical methods within the social sciences, as scholars have realized that many of the phenomena in which we are interested are complex and require deep inner reflection and equally penetrating examination. Quantitative approaches often cannot capture such phenomena well through their standard methods (e.g., self-report measures), so qualitative designs using interviews and other in-depth data-gathering procedures offer exciting, nimble, and useful research approaches.

Indeed, the number and variety of qualitative approaches that have been developed is remarkable. We remember Bill Stiles saying (quoting Chairman Mao) at one meeting about methods, "Let a hundred flowers bloom," indicating that there are many appropriate methods for addressing research questions. In this series, we celebrate this diversity (hence, the cover design of flowers).

The question for many of us, though, has been how to decide among approaches and how to learn the different methods. Many prior descriptions of the various qualitative methods have not provided clear enough descriptions of the methods, making it difficult for novice researchers to learn how to use them. Thus, those interested in learning about and pursuing qualitative research need crisp and thorough descriptions of these approaches, with lots of examples to illustrate the method so that readers can grasp how to use the methods.

The purpose of this series of books, then, is to present a range of different qualitative approaches that seemed most exciting and illustrative of the range of methods appropriate for social science research. We asked leading experts in qualitative methods to contribute to the series, and we were delighted that they accepted our invitation. Through this series, readers have the opportunity to learn qualitative research methods from those who developed the methods and/or who have been using them successfully for years.

We asked the authors of each book to provide context for the method, including a rationale, situating the method within the qualitative tradition, describing the method's philosophical and epistemological background, and noting the key features of the method. We then asked them to describe in detail the steps of the method, including the research team, sampling, biases and expectations, data collection, data analysis, and variations on the method. We also asked authors to provide tips for the research process and for writing a manuscript emerging from a study that used the method. Finally, we asked authors to reflect on the methodological integrity of the approach, along with the benefits and limitations of the particular method.

This series of books can be used in several different ways. Instructors teaching courses in qualitative research could use the whole series, presenting one method at a time as they expose students to a range of qualitative methods. Alternatively, instructors could choose to focus on just a few approaches, as depicted in specific books, supplementing the books with examples from studies that have been published using the approaches, and providing experiential exercises to help students get started using the approaches.

In this book, we present ideal-type analysis, a qualitative data analysis technique researchers may use to construct typologies. Emily Stapley, Sally O'Keeffe, and Nick Midgley ground the method in its sociological roots, clearly describe and illustrate the seven steps of ideal-type analysis, and base their discussion of the method's benefits and limitations on their own research experiences. This approach's particular strength is that it not only allows researchers to maintain a focus on the experiences of whole cases but also fosters the identification of patterns that emerge across the data set.

—*Clara E. Hill and Sarah Knox*

ESSENTIALS OF
Ideal-Type Analysis

1 CONCEPTUAL FOUNDATIONS

In this volume, we present an introduction to *ideal-type analysis*, a qualitative method for analyzing data to construct typologies in research. Because we are researchers working within the field of psychology and psychotherapy, many of the studies described in this volume are psychological research studies. However, the methodology presented here is transferable to other research contexts. Indeed, ideal-type analysis has its roots in sociological research.

In this first chapter, we begin by defining what a typology is, explaining how ideal-type analysis fits into the qualitative research tradition, and describing the philosophical and epistemological positions underpinning this approach. We then go on to identify the key features that distinguish the ideal-type analysis approach to provide sufficient context for the more detailed description later in this volume of the practical steps to be followed in conducting an ideal-type analysis.

https://doi.org/10.1037/0000235-001
Essentials of Ideal-Type Analysis: A Qualitative Approach to Constructing Typologies,
by E. Stapley, S. O'Keeffe, and N. Midgley

CONSTRUCTING TYPOLOGIES IN PSYCHOLOGY

A *typology* is an ordered set of categories that can be used to organize and understand objects and people according to their similarities and differences (Mandara, 2003). The creation of typologies is not new in psychology. Over decades of research, psychologists have developed typologies of such constructs as parenting styles (e.g., Baumrind, 1991; Simons & Conger, 2007), personality types (e.g., Bohane et al., 2017; Vollrath & Torgersen, 2002), and coping strategies (e.g., Aldridge & Roesch, 2008; Vandoninck & d'Haenens, 2015) in their efforts to understand human behavior. For example, once we are offered the distinction between "permissive," "authoritarian," and "authoritative" parenting styles (Baumrind, 1991), a shape and pattern are given to the infinite variety of ways in which parents behave. These can then be used to make predictions about the world. For instance, we can hypothesize that a child whose parents have an authoritarian parenting style may be less creative at school than a child whose parents have an authoritative parenting style (Mehrinejad et al., 2015).

Although all of us may implicitly be identifying types in our daily lives all the time (e.g., "She is an introvert," "She is an extrovert"), research allows us to systematize this process. A typology is formed on the basis of a grouping process, whereby cases or research participants are divided into different types or groups on the basis of their common features. Thus, typologies provide the means for psychologists to "identify, organize, and systematically describe naturally occurring behavioral patterns of people in such a way that the wholeness of the people is retained" (Mandara, 2003, p. 132). As a rule, when developing a typology, the characteristics within a type should be as similar as possible, and the differences between the types should be as distinct as possible, so that the cases within a type resemble each other and there is sufficient heterogeneity between the types (Kluge, 2000).

Several methods have been used to form typologies in psychology research, some of which belong to a more quantitative research tradition, whereas others are more aligned with a qualitative or mixed-methods research tradition. Such methods include cluster analysis, which is a multivariate statistical method (e.g., Clatworthy et al., 2005; Henry et al., 2005); Q-methodology (e.g., Cross, 2005; Flurey et al., 2016) and qualitative comparative analysis (e.g., Legewie, 2013; Rihoux, 2003), which are mixed-methods data analysis techniques; and ideal-type analysis, which is a qualitative data analysis method (e.g., Stuhr & Wachholz, 2001; Wachholz & Stuhr, 1999; Werbart et al., 2011, 2016). While the methodologies of these techniques and the types of data that they work with differ, at the heart of all these approaches is the desire to condense or render more manageable large amounts of data, to enable meaningful comparisons to be made across a data set, and to create systematic groupings within the data.

Despite the utility and prominence of typologies within psychology, there is, in fact, little methodological guidance available to explain the process of constructing a typology, particularly as a qualitative method for analyzing data (Kluge, 2000). Although typology creation could follow, for example, from conducting a narrative analysis (Sharp et al., 2018) or a framework analysis (Ritchie & Spencer, 1994), ideal-type analysis is an important addition to the family of qualitative research methods because it offers a systematic, rigorous methodological approach specifically for the development of typologies from qualitative data (Gerhardt, 1994). However, compared with such approaches as thematic analysis (Braun & Clarke, 2006) and interpretative phenomenological analysis (IPA; Smith et al., 2009), ideal-type analysis has, to date, been relatively rarely used within the field of qualitative psychology research. Usage thus far has perhaps been most common among psychotherapy researchers, who have sought to explore clients' experiences of and ideas about therapy, with implications for clinical practice (McLeod, 2011). We propose in this volume that ideal-type analysis provides a way of studying the psychological world that has great value and offers something different to other better-known qualitative methods.

HISTORICAL AND EPISTEMOLOGICAL UNDERPINNINGS OF IDEAL-TYPE ANALYSIS

Origins of Ideal-Type Analysis

The ideal-type approach originated in the work of Max Weber (1904), one of the early pioneers in the field of sociology, who argued against a narrowly positivist view of knowledge, believing that all social research has an interpretative component. Weber was interested in understanding and explaining historical and social phenomena, processes, and events, such as the links between capitalism and the "protestant ethic" (Psathas, 2005). In his investigations of such phenomena, Weber sought to bridge the gap between nomothetic approaches—those concerned with establishing general laws—and idiographic approaches—those tied to the individual experience and not intended to generalize beyond this (Psathas, 2005). Weber's answer was the ideal type: "An analyst's solution which was both general and specific" (Psathas, 2005, p. 149).

The ideal type, in Weber's thinking, was a description derived by a researcher from their observations of an empirical reality or a social phenomenon, as a first step in their analysis of a little-known or little-explored topic (Psathas, 2005; Swedberg, 2018). The ideal type was not intended to be a fully accurate and complete depiction of that particular reality or phenomenon; rather, it was intended to be an example, theory, or generalization of it (McIntosh, 1977; Psathas, 2005; Williams, 2002). Thus, the word "ideal" in an ideal-type context does not mean "perfect" or "best," but instead, it refers in the philosophical sense to an "idea" (McLeod, 2011; Werbart et al., 2016) or to "something that exists only in the mind" (Philips, Werbart, et al., 2007, p. 217)—a mental representation that will never be entirely identical with social reality but that helps to make such reality understandable.

For Weber, the ideal type was a "methodological tool" or "yardstick" for measuring similarities and differences between phenomena, processes, and events across time periods and places (Kvist, 2007; Psathas, 2005; Werbart et al., 2016). Essentially, the ideal type is an analytical construct or hypothesis about a particular phenomenon against which different instances or examples of that phenomenon can be measured, tested, and interpreted (Gerhardt, 1994; Stuhr & Wachholz, 2001; Wachholz & Stuhr, 1999; Werbart et al., 2016). Thus, the purpose of constructing the ideal type "is to obtain an adequate reduction of empirical data such that comparative analysis becomes possible" (Werbart et al., 2016, p. 929). Through a process of comparison, the researcher can use the ideal type, constructed in relation to a particular phenomenon, as a tool to enable interpretation and understanding of other similar phenomena (Gerhardt, 1994; Psathas, 2005) and to generate new ideas about reality (Swedberg, 2018).

Another sociologist, Uta Gerhardt (1994), later translated Weber's original methodology for forming and testing ideal types into a qualitative sociology research method: ideal-type analysis. Gerhardt's method reflects and partly extends Weber's original thoughts about ideal types (Stuhr & Wachholz, 2001; Wachholz & Stuhr, 1999). In the development of her methodology, Gerhardt reflected on the limitations that she had observed of existing qualitative research methods. Discussing approaches such as grounded theory and ethnographic research, she argued that they "either underestimate or overestimate the value of individual case evidence" (Gerhardt, 1994, p. 92). For instance, Gerhardt saw grounded theory as a process for generalizing across individual cases and, in doing so, losing touch with the diversity among individual cases. Moreover, for Gerhardt, the focus in ethnographic research on depicting social reality using an individual case came at the expense of systematically situating this case within a range of cases, which could offer further insight into that reality.

Consequently, in advocating ideal-type analysis, Gerhardt (1994) wanted to avoid, first, what she saw as the loss of individual case material in the process of generalizing across cases and, second, the sanctification of individual cases "into quasi absolute evidence of covert meaning spheres" (p. 94). Taking Gerhardt's approach to ideal-type analysis, the researcher would first summarize each participant's narrative (e.g., an interview transcript) so that each participant is represented as a "case reconstruction." The researcher would then compare the case reconstructions with each other to discern differences between participants and identify patterns or groupings of participants with similar experiences. Next, the researcher would select an ideal-typical case exemplar for each grouping, which would represent that grouping in a particularly "pure" or "optimal" form. Finally, the researcher would seek to explain the patterns they had found, such as by looking at the demographic or contextual characteristics of the participants within each grouping and by noting individual participants' similarities and differences with the ideal-typical case exemplar for each grouping.

Echoing Weber's (1904) earlier thinking, Gerhardt's (1994) ideal-type analysis approach was thus an attempt to bridge the gap between a focus on the individual case and a focus on the patterns arising across cases in qualitative data analysis while ensuring methodological rigor. Gerhardt's method for ideal-type analysis, originally developed as a qualitative sociology research method, has since also been applied in qualitative psychology research. (See Chapter 2, this volume, for a list of examples of studies using ideal-type analysis.) Psychology researchers have tended to retain a close connection with Gerhardt's original methodology but have also adapted and extended it, depending on their study aims and the kinds of data they have collected (McLeod, 2011).

Epistemology and Ideal-Type Analysis

Although Weber was a pioneer in his critique of positivist approaches to knowing and understanding the world, it has been argued that Weber never satisfactorily explained the epistemological basis for his work on the ideal type (McIntosh, 1977). However, in her work, Gerhardt (1994) saw the qualitative researcher as ultimately deriving knowledge through their interpretation of participants' subjective accounts. Thus, knowledge developed through qualitative data analysis can be seen as the product of both the participant's and the researcher's subjectivity. Yet, Gerhardt also championed the importance of the researcher taking a rigorous and systematic approach to their interpretations and saw ideal-type analysis as facilitating this. In terms of the different epistemological perspectives adopted by qualitative researchers, if we take Gerhardt's view on knowledge, ideal-type analysis fits readily with what has come to be called a critical realist perspective.

Knowledge, from a realist perspective, captures a true reflection of something that is happening in the world that we live in, such as a social or psychological process (Willig, 2012). This perspective rests on the assumption that "certain processes or patterns of a social or psychological nature characterize or shape the behavior or the thinking of research participants, and these can be identified and conveyed by the researcher" (Willig, 2012, p. 11). Not many researchers today would consider themselves realists, according to this definition, because it is generally recognized that there can be no such direct knowledge of the world. However, that is not to say that we need to abandon any hope of learning about the world. Critical realism is the most prominent variation in realist thinking in the social sciences (Maxwell, 2010). When taking a critical realist perspective, researchers accept that there is a real world that exists independently of their perceptions and constructions of it, yet also accept that their understanding of it is a construction from their perspective or point of view (Maxwell, 2010).

Carrying out an ideal-type analysis from a critical realist perspective would mean that the researcher sees the ideal types that they construct, in an attempt to describe reality as constructed by the participants under study, as being an interpretation of that reality, which the researcher also constructs from their perspective and view of the world. Therefore, if we take this epistemological perspective, we see the construction and content of each ideal type as being dependent on the point of view, experience, and knowledge of the researcher at that moment (Schutz, 1967). Thus, in light of this, we also see the features of each ideal type as being those that are selected and deemed significant, relevant, or essential from the perspective of its creator, the researcher (Psathas, 2005). This means, first, that different ideal types referencing the same phenomena may be legitimately constructed by different researchers and, second, that the ideal type cannot be considered apart from the context within which it was constructed (Frommer et al., 2004; Psathas, 2005).

Consequently, ideal-type analysis also fits readily with a constructivist epistemological perspective. From this perspective, data are seen as being coconstructed by the researcher and participant and shaped by their views and experiences, which are in turn shaped by their context, including their social and cultural backgrounds (Charmaz & Henwood, 2017).

A constructivist approach to grounded theory, for example, sees reflexivity as a core research activity, whereby the researcher seeks to examine how their worldviews, language, and privileges influence all aspects of the research process, including the interpretations that they make and the meanings that they derive from their data (Charmaz, 2017). Willig (2016) pointed out the compatibility of a constructivist perspective with a critical realist perspective. Specifically, despite constructivism often being seen as more aligned with a relativist perspective (i.e., the view that there is only ever a subjective reality), both constructivists and critical realists alike subscribe to the view of the existence of an independent reality and, though we cannot produce an objective account of it, we can try and interpret and understand it from our context (Willig, 2016).

Yet, the fact that ideal-type analysis may readily lend itself to a critical realist or constructivist epistemological perspective does not prohibit the researcher from, for instance, constructing a typology as an additional step in their data analysis following their use of another qualitative method with a different epistemological underpinning. For instance, Vachon et al. (2012) initially conducted an IPA, which is informed by an interpretative phenomenological perspective (Smith et al., 2009), to explore the perspectives of oncology and palliative care nurses on death proximity and finiteness, their spiritual-existential experience, and caring. As a further step in their interpretation of the data, the authors then developed a typology, using ideal-type analysis, to describe the patterns between the themes that they had derived through their IPA (Vachon et al., 2012). So, ideal-type analysis is not inextricably linked to a particular epistemological position. Ultimately, what is important in any ideal-type analysis study, as indeed with any qualitative research study in general, is that the researcher explicitly acknowledges and explains the epistemological perspective guiding their analysis at the outset and, if necessary, at each stage of their study.

SITUATING IDEAL-TYPE ANALYSIS WITHIN THE QUALITATIVE RESEARCH TRADITION

Data in qualitative research may consist of interview or focus group transcripts, observations, naturally occurring conversations, field notes, diaries, clinical case notes, and other textual or visual data sources. Qualitative researchers typically collect multiple accounts from participants about a phenomenon of interest and then seek to understand what such accounts mean (Ayres et al., 2003). Meaning is ultimately conveyed through a detailed, narrative research report of the researcher's description or interpretation of participants' perceptions, understandings, or experiences of a phenomenon (Smith, 2015). One decision that qualitative researchers have to make is whether to use a cross-case approach or a case study approach to make sense of their data set (Ayres et al., 2003; Gerhardt, 1994). Ideal-type analysis is in a unique position as a method that bridges the gap between these two traditions (Gerhardt, 1994).

What do we mean by cross-case analysis? In bringing order to qualitative data, researchers often seek to find similarities and differences within and across the data set, in terms of participants' views, opinions, and experiences. Strategies for analyzing qualitative data in this way typically involve coding and sorting text into units of meaning, and then when an idea occurs repeatedly across participants, it may be identified as a theme, pattern, or core category in the data (Ayres et al., 2003). Thematic analysis (Braun & Clarke, 2006) and grounded theory (Charmaz, 2006; Glaser, 1992; Strauss & Corbin, 1998) are frequently used examples of such strategies in qualitative psychology research.

However, an issue with a cross-case approach to qualitative data analysis is that when split into separate units of meaning or themes, data are often decontextualized, with particular instances (e.g., transcript extracts) separated from the individual cases (or whole transcripts) to which they belong (Ayres et al., 2003). Essentially, a theme might well appear in a number of different interviews with different individuals (e.g., "fear of closeness" in a thematic analysis of people's experiences of intimate relationships), but in analyzing the data in this way, we can lose sight of how a particular theme might form part of a wider narrative for any single individual. So, for one participant, the fear of closeness might be related to a childhood in which their parents were intrusive and overpowering, leaving them afraid of letting people get close; whereas for another participant, the fear of closeness might be linked to a wider narrative about being an immigrant and facing experiences of racism. Thus, cross-case approaches to qualitative data analysis, which identify themes across a group of participants, pose the risk of losing person-specific information, without which the experience or perspective of any individual participant cannot be fully understood (Ayres et al., 2003).

In contrast to cross-case approaches to qualitative data analysis, within-case (or case study) approaches focus on deriving meaning from an individual case or participant. These approaches involve the intensive study of a single unit (e.g., a person, an interview) to better understand a larger class of similar units, drawing on this one instance (Gerring, 2004). The case study approach allows the researcher to understand the aspects of experience that occur, not as separate units of meaning across a data set of multiple participants, but rather as a pattern of meaning within the account of an individual participant (Ayres et al., 2003). The use of case studies in psychology has spanned multiple areas of qualitative research. For example, case studies have been used to study individuals' lived experiences of Parkinson's disease (Bramley & Eatough, 2005), experiences of recovering from alcohol abuse (Rodriguez-Morales, 2017), and teachers' decision making about whether to leave the profession (Towers & Maguire, 2017).

However, a case study approach also has its limitations. For instance, it is not always clear how general inferences can be drawn on the basis of case studies (Bengtsson & Hertting, 2014). Indeed, it has been argued that this approach risks overestimating the value of individual case material (Gerhardt, 1994). This is because it does not involve systematically comparing an individual case with multiple cases, and therefore there is not the opportunity to reject the results arrived at through a single case study by comparison with other accounts of a phenomenon (Gerhardt, 1994). Thus, some authors propose that it is, in fact, impossible to generalize from case study research (King et al., 1994).

Overall, therefore, neither cross-case nor within-case approaches to qualitative data analysis may be entirely adequate alone to enable the researcher to understand an experience fully. Psychological data can best be understood both through its parts and as a whole (Ayres et al., 2003). Thus, approaches to qualitative data analysis are needed that seek to understand the individual account in its own context, while also seeking to illuminate the variation or patterns that can exist across individuals' experiences (Ayres et al., 2003). Ideal-type analysis is one such approach that fulfills this remit.

KEY FEATURES OF IDEAL-TYPE ANALYSIS

Ideal-type analysis offers something different from other qualitative methods because it provides a rigorous, step-by-step methodology for researchers to use specifically to develop typologies from qualitative data.

Key Feature 1: Rich Description of Groups of Participants

In ideal-type analysis, a typology consists of a number of different types or groupings of participants developed to address a specific research question. Each type or grouping represents a key similarity, or multiple similarities, in the thoughts, feelings, and behaviors of the participants within it. In their analysis, the researcher seeks to accurately and comprehensively describe the characteristic features of each type (Stoecker, 2003). Of course, not every participant within a certain type will perfectly reflect all the features of that type. For example, an individual could generally consider themselves an introvert, but in some circumstances, that individual may tend to be more of an extrovert, meaning that they do not always exactly reflect the characteristics of the introvert personality type. Thus, in ideal-type analysis, to guide their description of the types, the researcher selects an individual participant or "optimal case" in each type who particularly exemplifies and reflects the key characteristics of that type (Stuhr & Wachholz, 2001; Wachholz & Stuhr, 1999). The word "optimal" in this context is not intended to imply desirability but instead refers to the case that most epitomizes the core features of each type. So, the Italian fascist, Benito Mussolini, could be considered an "optimal" case of a dictator because he ruled autocratically, with no governing body to check his power, and used the secret police to restrict the personal freedoms of his people. But the fact that he may be considered an optimal example of a dictator does not imply that this is a good or desirable type of political leadership!

Key Feature 2: Comparisons Between Groups and Individuals

Each type, or grouping of participants with similar experiences or perspectives, in ideal-type analysis is formed through the systematic comparison of individual participants with each other. In this way, ideal-type analysis provides a means for the researcher to retain a focus on the individual participant's experience, as well as on the patterns that exist across the data set, including within and between groups in the data set (Werbart et al., 2016). Thus, ideal-type analysis can be considered a systematic form of person-centered, multi-case-study research (Werbart et al., 2016).

Key Feature 3: Ideal Types as Hypotheses About Human Thought and Behavior

The types formed through ideal-type analysis can be considered hypotheses about aspects of human behavior, experience, or perception, which are intended to be tested against and, in doing so, enhance our understanding of reality or a given psychological phenomenon (Lindner, 2006; Stuhr & Wachholz, 2001; Wachholz & Stuhr, 1999). This means that as new typologies are formed, new hypotheses are created about how a particular psychological phenomenon can be understood. In this way, typologies provide the potential to generalize beyond the sample under study (Williams, 2002). For instance, Lindner (2006) identified four ideal types (or groupings) of suicidal men in a sample of psychotherapy patients—"disconnected," "hurt," "stormy," and "object dependent"—which he suggested could then provide a framework, or a set of "clinically relevant hypotheses," to facilitate the assessment of other patients (p. 212). Specifically, these ideal types, developed from one sample of suicidal men in Lindner's study, could potentially be used by clinicians assessing other suicidal male patients to consider which ideal type any given patient reflects and what implications this may have for how they engage in treatment and for their level of suicidal risk.

Previous studies have also sought to test the predictive validity of the types that they have developed. For instance, Philips, Wennberg, and Werbart (2007) constructed a typology of people's ideas of cure before receiving psychotherapy. The authors hypothesized that people with an "approaching" idea of a cure, defined as facing your problems as a way of improving your capacity to manage them, would be less likely to end treatment prematurely than those who had a more distancing idea of cure, defined as avoiding your problems as a way of expending minimal effort in managing them. Likewise, attachment researchers, making use of Ainsworth and Bell's (1970) typology of preschool children's attachment types, have been able to make predictions about children's emotional well-being and academic success. For example, Jacobsen and Hofmann (1997) found that children with a "secure" type of attachment, as demonstrated in the Strange Situation test when they were toddlers, were more likely to thrive in middle childhood than those who, as toddlers, had shown a more "insecure" type of attachment.

Key Feature 4: Ideal-Type Analysis as a Form of "Qualitative Cluster Analysis"

Researchers have drawn comparisons between statistical cluster analysis and ideal-type analysis, with the latter being described as a form of "qualitative cluster analysis" (Kuckartz, 1991; Stuhr & Wachholz, 2001, p. 165). Indeed, both methods can be used to identify particular groups of people with shared characteristics, to enhance our understanding of the needs, experiences, and behaviors of different groups of people. For example, statistical cluster analysis has been used in health psychology to identify which groups of people are at risk of developing particular medical conditions, to enable the appropriate development and targeting of interventions (see Clatworthy et al., 2005). Likewise, ideal-type analysis has been used to identify how different groups of people engage with mental health services, with implications for the nature of effective support provision for these groups (e.g., O'Keeffe, Martin, Target, & Midgley, 2019; Stapley et al., 2017).

However, the two approaches also differ in several key ways. The type of data used in a statistical cluster analysis typically consists of numerical scores or codes. The variables by which cases are compared in a statistical cluster analysis are predefined ("top-down" or deductively) by the researcher before their analysis (Stuhr & Wachholz, 2001). This type of analysis is usually conducted using a statistical software package. However, the type of data used in an ideal-type analysis typically consists of qualitative data, and the process of creating types is "bottom-up" or inductive, starting with the researcher making sense of their (usually textual) data and then gradually identifying types on the basis of comparisons between participants. Thus, in an ideal-type analysis, unlike in a statistical cluster analysis, the variables that form the basis for any groupings have typically not been defined by the researcher before their analysis. This allows the researcher to remain open to the unexpected, and thus the researcher may identify groupings of similar cases on a basis that they did not know existed until they analyzed the data.

SUMMARY

The creation of typologies is not new in psychology, but there has been little methodological guidance available to explain the process of constructing a typology. Ideal-type analysis offers something different from thematic approaches to qualitative research or from ethnographic or case study research methods in that it provides a rigorous, step-by-step methodology for researchers to use to develop typologies from qualitative data. Ideal-type analysis has four key features:

- rich description of groups of participants
- comparisons between groups and individuals
- ideal types as hypotheses about human thought and behavior
- ideal-type analysis as a form of qualitative cluster analysis

Ideal-type analysis has its roots in the thinking and methodology of sociologists Max Weber (1904) and Uta Gerhardt (1994). Gerhardt's methodology for ideal-type analysis was originally developed as a qualitative sociology research method but has since also been applied in qualitative psychology research. In terms of the different epistemological perspectives adopted by qualitative researchers, ideal-type analysis fits readily (though not inextricably) with a critical realist or constructivist perspective.

2 DESIGNING THE STUDY AND COLLECTING THE DATA

In this chapter, we describe key aspects of the study design and data collection process that a researcher seeking to conduct an ideal-type analysis would need to consider.

WHAT RESEARCH QUESTIONS CAN IDEAL-TYPE ANALYSIS BE USED TO ANSWER?

The decision to use ideal-type analysis ultimately depends on the research aims of the study. Ideal-type analysis can be used to answer research questions that seek to construct a typology (or typologies) to

- examine definitions and perceptions of concepts;
- classify different types of experience, perspectives, and opinions; and
- compare different patterns of behavior, feelings, or thinking.

Take the topic of childhood obesity, for example. If a researcher was interested in exploring the lived experiences of children with obesity, they might

https://doi.org/10.1037/0000235-002
Essentials of Ideal-Type Analysis: A Qualitative Approach to Constructing Typologies, by E. Stapley, S. O'Keeffe, and N. Midgley

decide to do a thematic analysis of interviews with children with obesity to delineate the shared and contrasting elements in their experiences. If they were interested in understanding obesity as an individual experience, however, they might decide to carry out a single in-depth case study, drawing on an interview (or interviews) with one child. Yet, if they were interested in understanding how children can experience obesity, focusing on both the nuance of individual experience and group-level patterns, ideal-type analysis could be a suitable approach. This approach would enable the researcher to explore cross-group themes in the experience of obesity in the context of broader individual narratives of personal experience, thus maintaining both a within-case and a cross-case perspective.

"How," "why," and "what" research questions are all appropriate for ideal-type analysis. This is because it is an approach that enables rich description of what participants are saying, doing, thinking, and feeling, as well as providing an opportunity for interpretation, understanding, and explanation. Ideal-type analysis is also an approach that facilitates researchers in asking about and exploring change longitudinally (over time), such as whether psychotherapy patients' representations of their parents change over the course of therapy (Werbart et al., 2011). In addition, using ideal-type analysis, researchers can explore the links between quantitative outcomes data and the types or categories formed from qualitative data, such as whether certain types of patients who drop out from psychological therapy have poorer clinical outcomes than other types (O'Keeffe, Martin, Goodyer, et al., 2019). See Chapter 5 for an overview of some of the different ways in which researchers have used ideal-type analysis in their studies.

To date, ideal-type analysis has perhaps most often been used by psychotherapy researchers (McLeod, 2011), but the approach is suitable for many different fields of psychology (and other disciplines). Some examples of studies using ideal-type analysis include

- the experiences of parents living with and managing their child's mental health issues over time (Jungbauer et al., 2003; Stapley et al., 2017);

- how dental students experience and deal with stress (Dahan & Bedos, 2010);

- the perceptions and coping strategies of patients diagnosed with a severe physical illness (e.g., Koenigsmann et al., 2006; Langenbach et al., 2002);

- how school pupils handle tasks (Busse, 2005), participate in lessons (Gisslevik et al., 2019), and make choices about their future education (Grytnes, 2011);

- psychotherapy patients' recollections or perceptions of their therapist (Stuhr & Wachholz, 2001; Wachholz & Stuhr, 1999);

- changes from pre- to posttherapy in psychotherapy patients' views about therapy and depression (Valkonen et al., 2011), representations of their parents (Werbart et al., 2011), and representations of themselves (Werbart et al., 2016); and

- psychotherapy patients' pretherapy ideas of a cure and the links between such ideas and subsequent engagement in therapy, the therapeutic alliance, and therapeutic outcomes (Philips, Wennberg, & Werbart, 2007; Philips, Werbart, et al., 2007).

WHAT SIZE AND TYPE OF SAMPLE ARE APPROPRIATE FOR IDEAL-TYPE ANALYSIS?

For ideal-type analysis, a fairly large sample is required to allow the researcher to draw comparisons across groups of participants (Gerhardt, 1994; McLeod, 2011). Many studies using ideal-type analysis have had samples of 40 or more participants. It is important to note, though, that although there is no sample size considered to be the maximum for an ideal-type analysis, the researcher must consider the demands on their time and capacity that conducting an ideal-type analysis with an extremely large sample (e.g., over 100 participants) would necessitate.

The number of cases within each ideal type or grouping derived from the data set during an ideal-type analysis will vary. For example, in a study of parents' experiences of managing their teenage child's depression and engaging with mental health services, Stapley et al. (2017) identified three ideal types from their data set, with the number of cases in each grouping ranging from six to 12. However, should a single grouping contain just one case or the majority of cases within a data set, though not implausible, this should encourage the researcher to check that the groupings that they have identified sufficiently represent their data set as a whole and capture the range of experiences and perspectives within it.

Heterogeneity within the sample is considered a benefit in ideal-type analysis in providing the researcher with enough variation between individuals to enable them to derive groupings of participants on the basis of their similarities and differences (Gerhardt, 1994). For instance, Werbart et al. (2016) sought to achieve maximal sample variation in their ideal-type analysis study, specifically in relation to participant age, gender, and housing area, and so used both respondent-driven sampling and purposive sampling methods to ensure that their sample included variation in participant characteristics. This contrasts with the preference for a relatively small, homogenous sample taken, for example, in an interpretative phenomenological analysis (IPA), where the aim is to understand the experience of a particular phenomenon among a small group who all share an experience (Smith et al., 2009).

A large data set can also create valuable opportunities over the course of an ideal-type analysis for the researcher to test their developing typology against different subsets of the data to facilitate and refine its development (see Chapter 6 for further details about how this could work in practice). For instance, in a study with 60 participants, data from the first 20 participants could be used to develop an initial typology, which could then be tested and refined using data from a further 20 participants. Then, if the typology seems to be robust on the basis of this, an independent researcher could also be asked to test the fit of the typology using the data from the final 20 participants, as an additional check on the credibility of the typology. Thus, akin to the grounded theory concept of theoretical saturation (see Charmaz & Henwood, 2017), it may be appropriate in some ideal-type analysis studies for sampling to end when no new types need to be added to the typology to represent additional data adequately.

WHAT DATA DO I NEED TO COLLECT FOR IDEAL-TYPE ANALYSIS?

Deciding what kind of data to collect is an important issue for anyone designing a research study. Some types of qualitative data analytic strategies are specific about what kind of data should be used. For example, as IPA mostly focuses on exploring people's lived experiences of a phenomenon, it tends to make use of in-depth interviews (Smith et al., 2009), whereas other approaches, such as conversation analysis, are designed for analyzing speech and language use in naturally occurring speech or conversation (Sidnell & Stivers, 2013). In contrast, ideal-type analysis was not developed for analyzing any specific type of qualitative data, making it flexible in terms of the kinds of qualitative data that can be used with it, including interview or focus group transcripts, observations, field notes, diaries, clinical case notes, and other sources of textual or visual data. Thus, the method of qualitative data collection for a study using ideal-type analysis should ultimately be informed by the research aims. Some examples of commonly used qualitative data sources in ideal-type analysis studies are given next.

Interview Data

Interview data have been frequently used in ideal-type analysis studies (McLeod, 2011). This may be because such studies have often been concerned with seeking to understand participants' experiences of certain phenomena, such as the experience of receiving a diagnosis of leukemia (Koenigsmann et al., 2006) or the experience of parenting a child with schizophrenia (Jungbauer et al., 2003), and such experiential research topics lend themselves to in-depth interviews as a method of data collection. An in-depth interview is essentially a "conversation with a purpose" between a participant and the researcher (Burgess, 1984). It is the researcher's job to support the participant to tell their story, related to the research aims, in their own words. Interviews should ideally be audio or video recorded and then transcribed verbatim because this provides the richest data for subsequent analysis.

In-depth interviews can be structured, semistructured, or unstructured. Semistructured interviews are the most commonly used form of interview in qualitative research (DiCicco-Bloom & Crabtree, 2006). In a semistructured interview, the researcher typically uses an interview schedule or a topic guide to facilitate their conversation with the participant (Kallio et al., 2016). An example of a semistructured interview schedule developed to explore young people's expectations of therapy can be seen in Exhibit 2.1. The interview schedule tends to be structured by broad questions of inquiry relating to the researcher's key areas of interest but also includes follow-up prompts

---

EXHIBIT 2.1. Example of a Semistructured Interview Schedule Devised by Midgley et al. (2011) to Explore Young People's Expectations of Therapy

1. **What brought you to seek help at this point in your life?**[a]
   - *Was it your own idea to seek help, or were others involved? Who?*

2. **Do you have your own ideas about what you think can help with your difficulties?**
   - *What do you think would need to happen for things to get better?*

3. **What are you expecting to happen when you meet with a therapist?**
   - *Have you met with a therapist before? What was that like?*
   - *What do you think will happen in your therapy sessions?*

4. **What do you hope will come out of going to therapy?**
   - *What kind of things do you hope will be different?*
   - *If you could fast-forward a year, what do you hope things will be like?*

---

[a]The key areas of research interest, or primary interview questions, are in bold. The follow-up prompts, or secondary interview questions, used to elicit more detail as necessary in relation to these key areas, are italicized.

to facilitate participants in telling their story in relation to these key areas. For instance, in a study where the key area of research interest is the experience of aging, it might also be important for the researcher to prompt participants to tell a fuller story about this that includes their sense of who they are and how they have developed over the life course. This would then allow the researcher to understand any themes arising regarding the experience of aging in the context of each participant's life story.

Observations and Naturally Occurring Data

Another approach to data collection that has been used in ideal-type analysis studies is the observation of naturally occurring events, such as therapy sessions (Lindner, 2006), school classes (Gisslevik et al., 2019), or the implementation of an intervention (Riley & Hawe, 2009). Such studies have used audio or video recordings of interactions or events, field notes, diaries, and clinical case notes as sources of qualitative data for analysis. However, whereas use of numerically coded observational data would be typical in a statistical cluster analysis, for an ideal-type analysis, such data should consist of rich and detailed textual or visual information.

Observing interactions can be advantageous for an ideal-type analysis aiming to explore how people behave in a particular situation. For example, Gisslevik et al. (2019) sought to characterize how pupils participated in and responded to education about sustainable food consumption and delineate the factors that influenced pupils' goal achievement opportunities in this subject. For such a study, simply interviewing the pupils would have given the authors relatively minimal information about how the pupils engaged with the subject. So, the authors audio and video recorded the pupils working in lessons, transcribed the recordings, wrote observational field notes during lessons, and collated pupils' answers in written assignments and tests. The authors then conducted an ideal-type analysis to form groupings of pupils with similar characteristics or ways of participating in the lessons.

Ethical Considerations in Qualitative Data Collection

Ethical approval must be sought in accordance with the guidelines from your research institution before you begin data collection for any research study. The use of interview, observational, and naturally occurring data collection methods in qualitative research requires important consideration of the issue of informed consent (Byrne, 2001). Through provision of a comprehensive information sheet and consent form, all participants must be fully informed about the purposes, nature, and procedures of the research and understand how their data will be collected, used, and stored, including the provision of consent to be audio or video recorded. Participants typically give their informed consent at the outset of the research through signing a consent form in written, digital, or verbal form (see Byrne, 2001, for further information about the process of seeking informed consent from qualitative research participants). The use of audio or video recording in qualitative research also brings about a number of practical challenges, such as procuring equipment with an appropriate level of security or encryption and storage capacity, ensuring the quality of recording, and enabling the secure transfer to and storage of data at the research institution.

Confidentiality is a cornerstone of the researcher–participant alliance in all forms of research (Sanjari et al., 2014). Participants agree to provide the researcher with an insight into their feelings, perspectives, and experiences under the premise that the things they say will remain confidential or private between them and the research team. However, ensuring complete confidentiality can be challenging in qualitative research, especially with an approach such as ideal-type analysis, where the features of a particular case may need to be presented in some detail. Thus, the researcher should take steps to ensure that the anonymity and confidentiality of participants are maintained and openly inform or discuss with participants at the outset of the research how this will be achieved. For instance, one step might be to remove or disguise any overtly identifying details within transcripts (e.g., names of people and places) before the inclusion of quotations in any report of the findings. In some cases, it may also be important to return to participants with a preliminary draft of the study findings before publication to ensure that they feel that their anonymity has been suitably protected.

DO I NEED A RESEARCH TEAM TO BE ABLE TO CONDUCT IDEAL-TYPE ANALYSIS?

Collaborating, discussing, and reflecting on one's process and findings with others tend to be of benefit in qualitative research (Milford et al., 2017). Ideal-type analysis is no exception to this. A team approach can minimize the burden that may arise in collecting, transcribing, and analyzing large amounts of qualitative data. Research team members can also provide valuable feedback on a researcher's data collection or analysis process and their interpretations. The latter is useful both in terms of facilitating the refinement of the research process and as a check on the degree of influence of each researcher's preconceptions and biases throughout the research.

As with consensual qualitative research (Hill et al., 2005), the process of discussion and reaching a shared understanding is a core feature of a team approach to ideal-type analysis. Nonetheless, the role and extent of involvement of the research team members (e.g., fellow students, colleagues, academic supervisors) in conducting an ideal-type analysis can vary, for example, in terms of their remit in the analysis or the timing of their involvement. The initial stages of an ideal-type analysis (described further in Chapter 3) include such steps as familiarization with the data set and writing descriptions or summaries (case reconstructions) of each participant's data. These tasks could feasibly be conducted by one researcher or shared between members of the research team, with a clear protocol established for what these tasks entail.

In the next stages of an ideal-type analysis (described further in Chapter 3), the case reconstructions for all participants are systematically compared with each other to explore the similarities and differences between them as the basis for the formation of the ideal types or groupings of similar participants within the data set. One member of the research team could take primary responsibility for this process initially and then discuss emerging patterns of similar cases with other members of the research team to refine the process going forward (Stapley et al., 2017) or to finalize the descriptions and names of the ideal types (Stuhr & Wachholz, 2001; Wachholz & Stuhr, 1999). However, this stage of the analysis could also be enacted entirely through consensus-building discussions within the research team, with all members involved from start to finish in comparing and contrasting all the cases and deriving and describing the resultant typology (Jungbauer et al., 2003).

Overall, conducting an ideal-type analysis is typically not an entirely solo endeavor. Although a single researcher can carry out an ideal-type analysis, the approach benefits enormously from having a team involved (McLeod, 2011). However, the degree, timing, and purpose of the involvement of the research team, as well as who is involved, will ultimately depend on the feasibility of their involvement, such as in terms of their capacity and, if necessary, their expertise in the subject area or methodology.

HOW DO I MANAGE RESEARCHER SUBJECTIVITY IN IDEAL-TYPE ANALYSIS?

There have been debates within the qualitative methods literature about the role in the research process of the expectations, beliefs, and predispositions that the researcher holds and how these (and their influence) should be managed (if at all) as part of the research (Ortlipp, 2008; Roulston & Shelton, 2015). Some researchers have advocated for the bracketing of the researcher's prior beliefs, assumptions, and expectations entirely during the research process (Tufford & Newman, 2012). However, a constructivist approach to qualitative data analysis, such as Charmaz's (2006) constructivist approach to grounded theory, embraces the inevitability of subjectivity and views data collection, analysis, and interpretation as wholly co-constructed by the researcher and the participant, with its roots in the language, relationships, and "social, cultural, historical, and situational conditions of its construction" (Charmaz & Henwood, 2017, p. 3).

We argue that while researcher subjectivity is an inevitable influence during the research process, it is important that the researcher consciously and reflexively examines the expectations, assumptions, or biases that they bring to the research and is transparent to the reader about the potential influence of these on the research. A variety of methods have been proposed to aid the researcher in reflecting on and disclosing the impact of their assumptions on the data collection, analysis, and reporting process (Shenton, 2004). For example, the researcher could keep a reflective diary, in which to document, acknowledge, and make visible to the reader their experiences, opinions, and expectations over the course of the research (Ortlipp, 2008) or write memos or notes to capture their reflections throughout the analysis process (Charmaz & Henwood, 2017). Another method could involve asking a second researcher to reanalyze the data set or a proportion of the data set and, in doing so, act as a "critical friend" to the primary researcher, checking and challenging that their analysis is sufficiently grounded in the data.

A process akin to the latter has been employed in some studies using ideal-type analysis as a way of establishing the credibility or trustworthiness of a typology (e.g., Stapley et al., 2017; Werbart et al., 2011, 2016). Such credibility checks have tended to involve one or more independent researchers attempting to recategorize the interview transcripts or case reconstructions according to the descriptions of the ideal types developed by the original researcher(s). Discussions of instances of disagreement between the independent researcher(s) and the original researcher(s) can then lead to refinements being made as necessary to the typology, the cases (and their reconstructions) included within each type, and the descriptions of the types until consensus can be reached. However, in our methodology for ideal-type analysis (described in depth in Chapter 3), we see the intention of this credibility-checking process as being solely to provoke useful discussion and reflection, rather than as an attempt to establish interrater reliability or an assessment of the extent to which another researcher can interpret the data set in the same way as the original researcher. The latter is seen as impossible from both a critical realist and a constructivist epistemological perspective because "knowledge is always situated" (Willig, 2016, p. 7). For alternative views on this, see O'Connor and Joffe's (2020) discussion of the use of interrater reliability in qualitative data analysis.

In a study exploring the interactions between biography, the therapeutic relationship, and suicidality in 20 suicidal men entering into psychodynamic psychotherapy, Lindner and Briggs (2010) found that when two separate groups of researchers (one based in a therapeutic setting in Hamburg and one based in London) conducted an ideal-type analysis using the same data set, there were similarities and differences in the types formed by each group. For example, while each group had clustered the same cases together into types, they had given different labels and descriptions to the types. Lindner and Briggs felt that this could reflect the research groups' different theoretical and practice backgrounds, which varied by culture and training. Similarly, Armstrong et al. (1997) found that while the six qualitative research experts in their study ultimately derived similar themes from the same focus group transcript, how they reported and described these themes varied according to their different personal, contextual, and disciplinary perspectives.

Therefore, from studies like those of Lindner and Briggs (2010) and Armstrong et al. (1997), one could argue that "different ways of approaching the same subject [can] result in an increased understanding of complex phenomena," as opposed to "a failure of reliability" (Malterud, 2001, p. 484). In our view, credibility checks in ideal-type analysis (and indeed as part of other qualitative data analysis techniques) perhaps function best as a way of encouraging the researcher to (a) reflect on and make transparent any preconceived expectations they could have brought to and which could have influenced their analysis and (b) deepen their analysis through dialogue and consensus building. In this way, such checks are important not only in enhancing the trustworthiness of the process but also in enriching the content and rigor of the final analysis and results of the study. Multiple guidelines have been published for qualitative researchers to draw on to ensure and assess the methodological integrity of their research (e.g., Elliott et al., 1999; Levitt et al., 2018; Yardley, 2000), all of which are applicable for use in ideal-type analysis studies.

SUMMARY

The decision to use ideal-type analysis depends on the research aim(s) of the study. "How," "why," and "what" research questions are all appropriate for ideal-type analysis. Ideal-type analysis was not developed for any specific type of qualitative data, making it flexible in terms of the kinds of qualitative data that can be used with it. A fairly large sample is required for ideal-type analysis, and so, at the outset of their study, the researcher should consider how much data will be practical and possible to collect. Research ethics, the utility of research team involvement, and managing researcher subjectivity are all important issues to consider in any qualitative research study, for which ideal-type analysis studies are no exception.

3

ANALYZING THE DATA

In this chapter, we describe the steps taken to conduct an ideal-type analysis. To illustrate the process, we often refer to and use examples of studies using semistructured interviews. However, as explained in the previous chapter, ideal-type analysis can be conducted with a range of other textual and visual data sources, such as observations, field notes, diaries, and clinical case notes. Ideal-type analysis, as we describe here, is predominantly an inductive approach, whereby the ideal types are derived from the analysis in a "bottom-up" fashion, rather than being defined deductively or "top-down" beforehand. Our seven steps to conducting an ideal-type analysis are outlined in Exhibit 3.1.

The methodology we present in this chapter draws on, synthesizes, and expands on that originally outlined by the following authors: Gerhardt (1994); Lindner (2006); Lindner and Briggs (2010); Lindner et al. (2006); Philips, Werbart, et al. (2007); Stuhr and Wachholz (2001); Wachholz and

https://doi.org/10.1037/0000235-003
Essentials of Ideal-Type Analysis: A Qualitative Approach to Constructing Typologies,
by E. Stapley, S. O'Keeffe, and N. Midgley

EXHIBIT 3.1. The Seven Steps to Conducting an Ideal-Type Analysis

Step 1: Becoming familiarized with the data set
- Listening to audio recordings and reading transcripts
- Recording thoughts and observations

Step 2: Writing the case reconstructions
- Preparing a written summary for each case in the data set

Step 3: Constructing the ideal types
- Systematically comparing each case in the data set with each other to form clusters or groupings of similar cases (i.e., the "ideal types")

Step 4: Identifying the optimal cases
- Identifying a case that best represents each ideal type

Step 5: Forming the ideal-type descriptions
- Writing a comprehensive description of each ideal type, which delineates the characteristics of the optimal case and key features of other cases in that cluster

Step 6: Checking credibility
- An independent researcher attempts to regroup the cases into their ideal types, using the ideal-type descriptions

Step 7: Making comparisons
- Comparing cases within and between the ideal types and comparing the ideal types with each other

Stuhr (1999); and Werbart et al. (2011, 2016). Our methodology differs from these previous authors' in the following key ways:

- We advocate for an initial step at the outset of the analysis whereby the researcher familiarizes themselves with their data set before writing the case reconstructions.

- The construction of the ideal types is proposed as the third step in the analysis, which is completed in its entirety before identifying the optimal cases that most closely represent each ideal type.

- Forming the ideal-type descriptions is a distinct step in the analysis in its own right.

- Our approach formalizes the process of making comparisons within and between the ideal types as a final step in the analysis.

STEP 1: BECOMING FAMILIARIZED WITH THE DATA SET

To begin, the researcher familiarizes themselves with the data set to gain a sense of the content and extent of the material collected. This step reflects the first stage of a thematic analysis, as advocated by Braun and Clarke (2006). The researcher can achieve this in multiple ways, including

- conducting the interviews,
- listening to the audio files,
- transcribing the interviews,
- checking the accuracy of the transcripts, and
- reading and rereading the transcripts.

As part of this process, the researcher should record their thoughts and observations about the data set, which may be useful in their analysis later on. They should also reflect on and record any biases or preconceived ideas that they might bring to the analysis, which could influence their interpretation of the data. Such transparency is important in ensuring a clear audit trail for the data analysis process.

STEP 2: WRITING THE CASE RECONSTRUCTIONS

Case reconstruction, according to Gerhardt (1994), is the initial step in the ideal-type analysis process, whereby the researcher reconstructs or summarizes each participant's narrative as a "flow of events and actions covering the full observation period" (p. 97). In our approach, a case reconstruction is a written summary or description of the data for each participant that relates to the research question(s). Throughout this chapter, we use the word "case" to refer to a participant or a participant's case reconstruction. In an ideal-type analysis, the case reconstructions are typically the researcher's unit or object of analysis, as opposed to the raw data (e.g., the interview transcripts). Thus, for a sample of 40 interviews, the researcher would write 40 case reconstructions, one representing each participant's data.

Case reconstructions may be primarily descriptive, such as a description of the content of an interview transcript or the things that the participant says, but they can also include the researcher's comments, such as the researcher's interpretation of how the participant says things or the researcher's reactions or feelings while carrying out or listening to an interview. There may also be some initial attempt by the researcher to identify key aspects of the participant's experience or perspective within their case reconstruction. Ultimately, what is included in the case reconstruction depends on the research question(s). Parallels can be drawn between the case reconstruction process in ideal-type analysis and the concept of narrative construction in narrative analysis. The latter involves the researcher constructing narratives that represent each participant's individual story and "offer an understandable and credible explanation of the participants' experiences, including many examples in their own voices" (Sharp et al., 2018, p. 12).

An example of a case reconstruction from an ideal-type analysis study can be seen in Exhibit 3.2. To protect participant anonymity, the example included here has been created purely for illustrative purposes for this volume. It is written in the style adopted in a study aiming to explore, using ideal-type analysis, patterns in 63 adolescents' experiences of risk and protective factors in relation to their mental health and well-being (Eisenstadt, 2020; Eisenstadt et al., 2020). The 63 case reconstructions (one per participant) in this study aimed to give a description or summary of the entire content of each participant's interview. At the end of each case reconstruction, the lead author also listed their perception of the risk and protective factors experienced by the participant.

If one has multiple data sources, such as interviews and case notes, or multiple interviews for each participant, the case reconstruction for each participant could constitute a summary for that participant based on all of their available data, as shown in the example given in Exhibit 3.3. The case reconstruction in Exhibit 3.3 was one of 28 case reconstructions written for a study aiming to longitudinally explore, using ideal-type analysis, patterns in parents' experiences of managing their teenage child's depression and engaging with mental health services over a 2-year period (Stapley et al., 2017). The interviews were conducted with the parents in this study at three points: starting with their child's referral to child and adolescent mental health services (CAMHS)—Time 1; approximately 6 months later, or after their child's therapy at CAMHS—Time 2; and then again 1 year after that—Time 3. The case reconstructions in this study were succinct descriptions of the content of each participant's three interview transcripts. Thus, even though each participant's data in this study consisted of three interview transcripts, each participant was represented by just one case reconstruction, which summarized the content of their three interviews.

Case reconstructions could be written as separate documents or as separate rows in a spreadsheet. For ease in terms of the process of writing, reading, and sorting the case reconstructions into groups, the researcher could aim for each case reconstruction to be between one and four pages in length. However, ultimately the level of detail, amount of data, or proportion of the participant's interview(s) included in each case reconstruction is

EXHIBIT 3.2. Example of a Case Reconstruction Written to Represent the Content of One Interview Transcript. This Example Illustrates the Style Used in a Study of Adolescents' Experiences of Risk and Protective Factors in Relation to Their Mental Health and Well-Being (Eisenstadt, 2020; Eisenstadt et al., 2020)

The young person describes her experiences of being bullied in high school by a gang of girls. She reports having multiple physical and verbal altercations with the gang, which her teachers at school had ignored: "No one would help me. No one believed me when I told them what was happening." However, recently, she has received support from a school counselor, which has been helpful because the counselor has listened to her and has supported her in asking her teachers to take action against the gang. She is not sure how she ended up seeing the school counselor, but she is relieved that someone is "finally listening." The bullying has not completely stopped, but it is considerably less now than it was at the start of the school year.

Before seeing the school counselor, the only other person who had been supporting her was her mom. Her mom would give her advice about dealing with the bullying: "My mom told me to ignore them." Her mom had also phoned the school to tell the teachers about the bullying, but when the teachers had questioned the gang about it, they denied it. When asked how she handles the bullying now, the young person explains that she uses particular strategies, as suggested by her mom and the school counselor, to enable her to ignore the bullies and to calm down when she is feeling angry or stressed, such as taking deep breaths, counting to 10, or walking away: "I just leave the room, calm myself down, and then I go and tell a teacher. Teachers listen to me more now that my counselor and my mom have spoken to them."

In terms of her schoolwork, the young person reports that she finds Science hard, but Math is easier this year than it was last year. She thinks that this may be because she enjoys Math more this year. She finds it hard to concentrate in some lessons, particularly Science. Her grades are lower in Science this year than she would like them to be: "I want my Science grades to come back up." She asks her friends for help when she has difficulties with her Science homework. Her friends also tried to help her when she was being bullied, but there was not much that they could do because the gang bullied them too.

She has lots of friends whom she spends time with both inside and outside school. She enjoys hanging out with her friends, and they cheer her up when she is feeling sad: "They are always there for me, and I know that they will always be able to make me laugh if I'm ever feeling down." However, sometimes there are arguments within her friendship group, which can be difficult to deal with, particularly when she feels like she has to choose whose side to be on. So when arguments do happen between her friends, she tries to bring people back together by encouraging them to apologize to each other and see the other's point of view: "I don't like it when they fight, so I always try to make them calm down and speak to each other again."

Risk factors:
- bullying
- lack of support from teachers
- difficulties concentrating in lessons
- conflicts within friendship group

Protective factors:
- support from school counselor
- support from mom
- her repertoire of coping strategies
- positive relationships with friends

EXHIBIT 3.3. An Example of a Case Reconstruction Written to Summarize the Content of Three Interviews With One Participant Conducted at Three Points in Stapley et al.'s (2017) Study of the Experience of Being the Parent of an Adolescent Diagnosed With Depression

Interview 1: Point of Referral to CAMHS

Mom has noticed changes in her daughter's usual feelings and behaviors over the last 3 years. However, Mom (and their family doctor) did not realize that these changes were anything more than normal teenage feelings and behaviors until her daughter broke down and told her how depressed she had been feeling. Mom would like to be told by a professional at CAMHS how she should be parenting her daughter now and dealing with her depression. Mom is glad that her daughter will be receiving therapy but feels sad that this proves that there is something wrong with her.

Interview 2: Posttherapy at CAMHS

Mom thinks that her daughter's depression has improved as a result of her therapy at CAMHS, her growing maturity, and the provision of ongoing support from Mom. Mom's own therapist, whom she also worked with at CAMHS, taught Mom how to deal with her daughter's depression, gave her parenting advice, and was a source of emotional support for her as a parent. Mom's therapist also reassured her that her guilt in relation to the origins of her daughter's depression is unfounded and stated that she might never know what caused her daughter's depression.

Interview 3: One Year Later

Mom describes how her daughter's depression has continued to improve since she was discharged from CAMHS. Mom feels relieved and much less stressed now that her daughter is feeling so much better. Mom feels that her relationship with her daughter has improved because it is easier to parent her now that she is no longer depressed, she is more mature, and they have more in common. She will talk to Mom more readily about her feelings now. Mom thinks that her own therapy sessions at CAMHS indirectly helped her daughter because they helped Mom be calmer, a stronger parent, and better able to support her daughter. Mom feels well-equipped now to bring her other children through their teenage years.

Note. CAMHS = child and adolescent mental health services.

a decision to be made by the researcher and will depend on their research question(s) and the length or depth of their source material. Quotations from transcripts can be included in case reconstructions to illustrate points. Yet, it is important to bear in mind that the case reconstructions should typically be considerably shorter than the transcripts (or other source material) in length, given that they are intended to be a summary or description of the relevant data for each participant.

While writing the case reconstructions, the researcher should repeatedly read and reread each transcript and its corresponding case reconstruction alongside each other to check for any key missing details, inaccuracies, or interpretations that are not grounded in the data. The aim is to ensure that the case reconstructions are a fair reflection of all necessary content from the transcripts. A team approach, where researchers check and refine each other's case reconstructions, could be useful here. Having a standard structure for each case reconstruction may also ensure that all relevant material from each participant is included. For example, the researcher could first explore each interview transcript in relation to their research question(s) by giving brief descriptive labels (codes) to relevant transcript extracts. Then, each participant's case reconstruction could be structured according to the list of codes developed from their transcript, with associated descriptions and/or quotations of relevant transcript extracts also included (e.g., Philips, Werbart, et al., 2007; Werbart et al., 2011, 2016).

The case reconstructions could represent summaries of entire transcripts (e.g., as per Exhibit 3.2), or just the aspects of each transcript that are specifically relevant to the research question(s). An example of the latter can be seen in Stuhr and Wachholz's (2001) study of 49 patients' inner picture of their therapist 12 years after therapy. To formulate their case reconstructions, Stuhr and Wachholz first marked all the extracts in the interview transcripts that seemed relevant to the patient's perceptions of their relationship with their therapist. The authors then listed, verbatim, the extracts from each patient's transcript about their relationship with their therapist. An example of such a list from Stuhr and Wachholz's study can be seen in Exhibit 3.4. These lists were used as the basis for the case reconstructions to facilitate the authors in describing and judging how each patient referred to his or her therapist and what kind of image each patient had of their therapist.

EXHIBIT 3.4. Example of a List of Verbatim Extracts (Relevant to the Patient's Relationship With Their Therapist) Compiled From a Patient's Transcript in Stuhr and Wachholz's (2001, p. 159) Study Used as the Basis for the Patient's Case Reconstruction

"I remember her with pleasure"
"Mrs. A. was so nice and calm and quiet and warm"
"I really felt very good there"
"If Mrs. A. had said should we go on with the psychoanalysis, then I would have said okay"
"very calm"
"very understanding"
"a warm feeling"
"she should have intervened more"
"in the end you are on your own"

There are different ways in which the content of the case reconstructions could be organized. For example, each case reconstruction could consist of a summary of the entire content or relevant content of the transcript in chronological order (i.e., as it appears in the transcript), or it could be organized within the case reconstruction in a particular order. Exhibit 3.3 shows one approach, where each case reconstruction described relevant content from three interviews in the order in which they were conducted— from the point of referral to CAMHS, to posttherapy at CAMHS, and 1 year later. Such a chronological representation was felt to be necessary in Stapley et al.'s (2017) study to enable each participant's experience to be charted over the 2 years of the research project.

Another way of writing the case reconstructions could be to organize the content according to the domains the researcher is interested in. This may mean that data are not presented in a case reconstruction in the order in which they originally appeared in the transcript. For instance, O'Keeffe, Martin, Target, and Midgley (2019) carried out an ideal-type analysis to explore the reasons adolescents stopped attending therapy, which drew on a data set for which both adolescents and their therapists were interviewed about their experiences of therapy after the adolescents' therapy had ended. The content of the case reconstructions in their study was ordered according to three predetermined areas of interest: how the adolescent came to be referred for therapy, the story of therapy, and how therapy ended. The data for each participant were summarized in their case reconstruction within these three areas, regardless of where the data appeared in their transcripts.

STEP 3: CONSTRUCTING THE IDEAL TYPES

Once the case reconstructions are complete, they are used to form the ideal types. To do this, the researcher systematically compares and contrasts each case reconstruction with each other. The aim of this step is to explore the similarities and differences between whole cases (participants) in terms of the content of the case reconstructions, with the intention of identifying patterns across the data set and forming groupings (or ideal types) of similar cases (Gerhardt, 1994). What the researcher is looking for, in terms of the similarities and differences between cases, should be defined by the research question(s) under study. For instance, if the researcher were interested in exploring participants' ways of coping with mental health problems, the case reconstruction for each participant would capture the coping strategies they reported using. Then, during this third step, the researcher would be looking for similarities and differences between the case reconstructions in terms of participants' coping strategies, to devise ideal types or a typology of participants' ways of coping with mental health problems. Comparisons can be drawn here with grounded theory's constant comparative approach (Glaser, 1992), whereby cases, data, interpretations, and emerging patterns are repeatedly compared with each other to generate conceptually useful categories (e.g., Charmaz & Henwood, 2017; Walker & Myrick, 2006).

To aid the process of comparing and contrasting the cases in ideal-type analysis, the researcher might want to use paper copies of the case reconstructions and physically sort the paper copies into piles of similar cases. The advantage of doing this is that it enables the researcher to view their data set as a whole and easily move the cases from group to group. However, this may not be practical if the study has a large sample. In the latter situation, the case reconstructions could instead be sorted electronically, such as through cutting, pasting, and grouping the case reconstruction documents into different folders on a computer. See Exhibit 3.5 for an example of how such an electronic sorting process could look in practice.

Typically, this case sorting process would be applied to the entire data set from the outset. However, it can be helpful, particularly when working with large data sets, to carry out this process on a proportion of the data set initially. The researcher could then test their initial typology, developed

EXHIBIT 3.5. An Example of How the Researcher Could Sort the Case Reconstructions Electronically by Cutting and Pasting the Case Reconstruction Documents (One per Participant) Into Different Computer Folders (One per Ideal Type)

Name	^	Date Modified	Size	Kind
▼ 📁 Ideal type 1		Today at 15:19	--	Folder
📄 Case reconstruction 1.docx		26 May 2015 at 13:45	19 KB	Micros...(.docx)
📄 Case reconstruction 3.docx		26 May 2015 at 13:47	18 KB	Micros...(.docx)
📄 Case reconstruction 5.docx		26 May 2015 at 13:49	19 KB	Micros...(.docx)
📄 Case reconstruction 6.docx		26 May 2015 at 13:51	18 KB	Micros...(.docx)
📄 Case reconstruction 12.docx		26 May 2015 at 13:48	19 KB	Micros...(.docx)
📄 Case reconstruction 13.docx		26 May 2015 at 13:51	18 KB	Micros...(.docx)
▼ 📁 Ideal type 2		Today at 15:20	--	Folder
📄 Case reconstruction 4.docx		26 May 2015 at 14:31	18 KB	Micros...(.docx)
📄 Case reconstruction 7.docx		26 May 2015 at 15:34	19 KB	Micros...(.docx)
📄 Case reconstruction 10.docx		26 May 2015 at 15:32	19 KB	Micros...(.docx)
▼ 📁 Ideal type 3		Today at 15:20	--	Folder
📄 Case reconstruction 2.docx		1 Jun 2015 at 19:23	19 KB	Micros...(.docx)
📄 Case reconstruction 8.docx		26 May 2015 at 17:28	20 KB	Micros...(.docx)
📄 Case reconstruction 9.docx		26 May 2015 at 16:39	19 KB	Micros...(.docx)
📄 Case reconstruction 11.docx		31 May 2015 at 18:43	19 KB	Micros...(.docx)

from this proportion of the data set, against another proportion of the data set, by sorting or categorizing the new proportion of cases according to the ideal types that they developed from the initial proportion of cases. This process could help the researcher establish how robust or comprehensive their typology is relatively early on in their analysis process and determine whether it requires refinement (e.g., the addition of new types) to capture the experiences of new cases. This approach was taken in a study by O'Keeffe, Martin, Target, and Midgley (2019) and is described further in Chapter 6.

The case sorting process can be conducted as a team, whereby clusters of similar cases are identified through team discussion and agreement (e.g., Jungbauer et al., 2003; Lindner, 2006). For example, in their study of the experiences of the subjective burden of parents of children with schizophrenia, Jungbauer et al. (2003) used a consensus-building discussion within the research team to first identify individual cases within the data set that were particularly different from one another ("maximum contrasting"). These individual cases then served as the starting point for the authors' creation of preliminary categories into which the other case reconstructions, with similar experiences of subjective burden to these individual cases, were sorted. These categories, refined through ongoing team discussions throughout the case sorting process, ultimately became the ideal types in Jungbauer et al.'s study.

The case comparison process results in the researcher deriving various ideal types or groupings of similar cases from their data set, which should be homogenous or similar within themselves but distinct or different from each other (Stuhr & Wachholz, 2001; Wachholz & Stuhr, 1999). Within each grouping, not all cases will have had the same experience or share every feature of that particular "type," but there must be something fundamental (related to the research question or questions under study) about the cases within each grouping that links or groups them together as apart or separate from the other groupings of cases. While cases may have characteristics that resemble multiple ideal types, each case should only belong to one ideal type.

Consequently, a particular challenge is the potential event of "borderline cases," for which it is not at first clear which ideal type they should be part of or whether an additional ideal type needs to be formed to accommodate such cases (Gerhardt, 1994; Stuhr & Wachholz, 2001; Wachholz & Stuhr, 1999). Decisions need to be made about whether to subsume such cases within the existing groupings that they most closely resemble (albeit to a lesser or more marginal degree than the cases already classified within those groupings) or whether to collect more data to explore whether these cases, in fact, represent a distinct pattern in their own right (Gerhardt, 1994). In deciding how to deal with borderline cases, it is necessary for the researcher to remain open and reflective about the decisions that they made in terms of classifying each case into a particular ideal type in the first place.

For example, in a study of preschool children's attachment types, Ainsworth and Bell (1970) used observation data from a Strange Situation test to construct a coding frame for understanding different types of attachment behavior. This study did not draw on ideal-type analysis in its methodology but is relevant for illustrative purposes here in terms of how the research team handled cases that did not seem to fit into any of their existing types. As the research team observed how each child responded to being separated from and then reunited with their primary caregiver, they outlined the necessary conditions or core criteria that, if fulfilled, meant that a child would be classified as one of three attachment types: secure, insecure avoidant, or insecure preoccupied. The research team stipulated that a child must have met all core criteria for a particular attachment type to be classified as belonging to that type, which helped clarify and systematize their decision making during the case classification process. However, there was a certain group of children who did not appear to quite fit any of the existing three attachment types. These children were at first considered as "atypical" or discrepant cases but were then later understood through the identification of a new type, the "insecure-disorganized" attachment pattern (Main & Solomon, 1990). For this type, the defining characteristics, or necessary conditions for classification as that attachment type, were precisely the lack of any organized way of responding to the separation–reunion task. This example shows how reflection on borderline cases and whether these cases represent an additional type or can be subsumed within existing types can often lead to greater refinement of the typology itself.

A team approach to analysis may also be helpful in considering how to manage cases that do not quite fit into any of the existing types or have features that may belong equally to more than one type. This could involve reaching consensus within the team about where particular cases best fit (Stuhr & Wachholz, 2001; Wachholz & Stuhr, 1999). For example, Stapley et al. (2020) sought to explore changes in young people's well-being over two interviews over a 2-year period, in terms of whether the young people reported experiencing positive changes in their lives, relationships, and feelings over time (Category 1); negative changes (Category 2); or a mixture of positive and negative changes (Category 3). This study was not a typical ideal-type analysis study because the intention was not to identify types of change in participants' experiences bottom-up from the data set, but rather to explore participants' experiences within the context of the three categories of change described previously, which were prescribed or imposed top-down on the data set by the research team. However, this study did include a case reconstructions step in its methodology and involved a case sorting process, which makes it relevant here. Each participant in this study was represented by one case reconstruction, which summarized the content of their two interviews from Years 1 and 2 of the study. Two members of the research team separately categorized each case construction to one of the three categories. When the two researchers disagreed on which category the case reconstruction belonged to, a third member of the research team was then asked to categorize the case reconstruction to enable a majority consensus verdict to be reached. The researchers recorded their decisions in a spreadsheet (see Exhibit 3.6), along with their notes about their decision-making process, which provided an audit trail during the case reconstruction sorting process.

There is no minimum or maximum requirement for the number of ideal types identified from the data set during this step, although Werbart et al. (2016) advised that the researcher should strive "for a cluster solution with a minimal amount of clusters and mutually exclusive ideal types" (p. 930). For instance, in their study of parents' experiences of managing their teenage child's depression and engaging with mental health services over a 2-year period, Stapley et al. (2017) identified three ideal types of parental

EXHIBIT 3.6. Illustrative Extract From a Spreadsheet Designed to Capture the Research Team's Decision-Making Process During the Case Reconstruction Sorting Stage of the Qualitative Analysis Conducted in Stapley et al.'s (2020) Study

Case reconstruction ID	Researchers		
	Researcher 1	Researcher 2	Researcher 3
001	Positive	Positive	Not applicable
002	Positive	Mix of positive and negative	Positive
003	Mix of positive and negative	Mix of positive and negative	Not applicable
004	Mix of positive and negative	Negative	Negative
005	Negative	Mix of positive and negative	Negative

Note. This study involved deciding whether young people had experienced positive, negative, or a mixture of positive and negative changes in their well-being over time. The shading indicates shared reviewer opinion.

experience: the "learning curve" parents ($n = 12$ participants), the "finding my own solutions" parents ($n = 6$ participants), and the "stuck" parents ($n = 10$ participants). However, in a study of the changes in 41 men's and women's representations of their mothers and fathers from pretherapy to posttherapy to long-term follow-up, Werbart et al. (2011) identified 26 ideal types of participants' representations of their parents. It is important to note, however, that a large number of ideal types may make the case comparison process more unwieldy and difficult to manage, given that the researcher has to try and hold all the different ideal types in mind when deciding to which type each case reconstruction belongs. We suggest, therefore, that researchers using ideal-type analysis should seek to establish a parsimonious solution for their data to provide conceptual clarity in relation to their research question(s).

STEP 4: IDENTIFYING THE OPTIMAL CASES

Having developed the ideal types through comparing the case reconstructions with each other in Step 3, the researcher then identifies a single case reconstruction per ideal type, which best illustrates that pattern of similar cases or which captures the essence of that ideal type in a particularly pure or "optimal" form (Lindner, 2006; Stuhr & Wachholz, 2001; Wachholz & Stuhr, 1999). As Gerhardt (1994) described it, this case "is the most clearcut (if not slightly overdrawn) example for the type area concretizing the respective pattern" (p. 100). Optimal cases have also been referred to in the literature as "prototypes" (Lindner, 2006; Lindner & Briggs, 2010; Lindner et al., 2006). An example of an optimal case is presented in Exhibit 3.7. This optimal case (a mother and a father) exemplified the "finding my own solutions" ideal type in Stapley et al.'s (2017) study and was deemed to be most representative of this particular pattern of parental experience out of the six cases in total who had been identified as exhibiting this pattern.

Stapley et al.'s (2017) rationale for selecting this case as the optimal case for the "finding my own solutions" ideal type was as follows. As shown in Exhibit 3.7, in their first interview (pretherapy), the parents described the solutions they had already given their daughter for managing the symptoms of her depression while waiting for her referral to CAMHS. In their second interview (posttherapy), the parents discussed their dissatisfaction with CAMHS and how little they felt it had helped and alluded to their own solutions that they already had for dealing effectively with emotional problems. In their third interview (1 year later), the parents talked about the

EXHIBIT 3.7. The Optimal Case (Presented in Its Case Reconstruction Form) That Characterized the "Finding My Own Solutions" Ideal Type in Stapley et al.'s (2017) Study

The optimal case for the "finding my own solutions" ideal type was Mr. and Ms. Woods.[a]

Interview 1: Point of Referral to CAMHS

At the point of their daughter's referral to CAMHS, the Woods hope that their daughter's therapist will be somebody whom their daughter can talk to and who will give their daughter some coping strategies, as well as "sensible" feedback and suggestions that "are not too far different" from those that they, as her parents, have already given her.

Interview 2: Posttherapy at CAMHS

Following their daughter's therapy at CAMHS, the Woods state that their daughter's emotional difficulties are still ongoing, primarily as a result of the issues that she is still experiencing academically and socially at college. The Woods do not feel that their daughter's therapy has been helpful for her because her therapist has been unable to engage with her. After a small number of therapy sessions, their daughter decided that she did not want to go to CAMHS anymore. The Woods also do not feel that the small number of therapy sessions that they had attended separately at CAMHS had been necessary or helpful either. According to Ms. Woods, "I've always had family and friends give me reality checks."

Interview 3: One Year Later

A year later, Mr. and Ms. Woods state that their daughter is no longer experiencing any difficulties, which has been a big source of relief and happiness for them as parents. The Woods see this improvement as being primarily due to their daughter's new college, which they have recently moved her to and where she is "thriving." Mr. and Ms. Woods state that, ultimately, they just kept trying, through a process of trial and error, until they found a way to solve the problem of their daughter's difficulties. As Ms. Woods explains, "And you've got to go back to the drawing board and think 'How else am I going to tackle it?' and keep going until you find, you know, a solution or something that helps."

Note. CAMHS = child and adolescent mental health services. From "The Journey Through and Beyond Mental Health Services in the United Kingdom: A Typology of Parents' Ways of Managing the Crisis of Their Teenage Child's Depression," by E. Stapley, M. Target, and N. Midgley, 2017, *Journal of Clinical Psychology, 73*(10), pp. 1434–1435 (https://doi.org/10.1002/jclp.22446). Copyright 2017 Wiley Periodicals, Inc. Reprinted with permission.
[a] A pseudonym.

improvements they had noticed in their daughter's depression, which they ascribed to the solutions that they had ultimately found themselves to help their daughter. Essentially, compared with the other cases in the "finding my own solutions" ideal type, all of whom had had relatively similar experiences, this case particularly exemplified the core elements of this pattern of experience—including that, in all three of their interviews, the parents alluded to their feeling that it was up to them to find their own effective solutions for their child's difficulties.

The purpose of identifying the optimal case for each ideal type is that this case then becomes the orientation point to which the researcher compares all of the other cases and considers in what ways and to what extent other cases deviate from or reflect the optimal case (Philips, Werbart, et al., 2007; Stuhr & Wachholz, 2001; Wachholz & Stuhr, 1999; Werbart et al., 2011, 2016). The process of comparing cases with the optimal case within each ideal type enables the researcher to thoroughly explore the experiences and perspectives of all the participants who represent each ideal type in their analysis. The optimal case also guides the researcher's writing of their description of the ideal type to which it belongs because it epitomizes it (Stuhr & Wachholz, 2001; Wachholz & Stuhr, 1999).

It is important to note here that other authors have alternatively identified the optimal cases at an earlier stage in their analysis as an initial step in their construction of the ideal types (e.g., Philips, Werbart, et al., 2007; Stuhr & Wachholz, 2001; Wachholz & Stuhr, 1999; Werbart et al., 2011, 2016). An advantage of their approach is that those cases designated early on in the analysis process as optimal cases, due to their extreme differences from each other, can then provide a useful starting point from which to proceed with the case sorting process for the remaining cases. For example, starting from the optimal case, the researcher can then search for others with similar experiences, which can then be sorted within that emerging grouping (Lindner, 2006; Lindner & Briggs, 2010). However, in our methodology, we advocate for identifying the optimal cases after constructing the ideal types because our view is that once the ideal types are formed, the identification of the optimal case then formalizes the core characteristics of that grouping. Moreover, we see it as advantageous to consider all cases equally within each grouping before identifying the case that best characterizes that group.

STEP 5: FORMING THE IDEAL-TYPE DESCRIPTIONS

Having identified an optimal case for each ideal type, the researcher then seeks to construct a detailed description of and develop a name for each of the ideal types. By keeping the optimal case for each ideal type in mind, the researcher can formulate an ideal-type description that represents this case and, in doing so, characterizes the ideal type or grouping of similar cases to which it belongs (Stuhr & Wachholz, 2001; Wachholz & Stuhr, 1999). Not all the cases within the grouping (including the optimal case) will necessarily reflect every aspect of the ideal-type description, but each will represent it to a greater or lesser extent (Kühnlein, 1999). As previously described, from interviews with 28 parents at three times about their experiences of managing their teenage child's depression and engaging with mental health services over a 2-year period, Stapley et al. (2017) identified three ideal types of parental experience. The descriptions developed by the authors for these three ideal types are shown in Exhibit 3.8.

The optimal case for Ideal Type 2 in Stapley et al.'s (2017) study, the "finding my own solutions" parents, was shown in Exhibit 3.7. The majority of the characteristics of the ideal-type description for this grouping, as presented in Exhibit 3.8, were reflected in the optimal case in Exhibit 3.7, apart from the following sentence in Exhibit 3.8: "and have clear ideas about the origins of these difficulties." This sentence, while not reflected in the optimal case, was reflected in other cases assigned to this ideal type, which is why it was ultimately included in the ideal-type description for this grouping. Thus, looking at Exhibits 3.7 and 3.8, it is possible to see how,

EXHIBIT 3.8. Ideal-Type Descriptions Developed to Represent Three Ideal Types of the Experience of Parenting an Adolescent With a Diagnosis of Depression in Stapley et al.'s (2017) Study

Ideal Type 1: The "Learning Curve" Parents
The parents in this group recognize that their child has been experiencing difficulties, although they are often unsure about how significant these difficulties potentially are. Nonetheless, they see the value of seeking professional help for both them and their child. These parents then tend to find the help that they receive from professionals at CAMHS to be life-changingly helpful for both them and their child, as they develop a new perspective over time in relation to their child's difficulties and/or in relation to themselves as parents and adapt accordingly.

Ideal Type 2: The "Finding My Own Solutions" Parents
The parents in this group generally recognize that their child has been experiencing difficulties and have clear ideas about the origins of these difficulties. Although these parents initially see value in seeking professional help for their child, they then tend to express their disappointment in CAMHS and report that they end up finding their own solutions to their child's difficulties instead.

Ideal Type 3: The "Stuck" Parents
The parents in this group recognize that their child has been experiencing difficulties and see the value of seeking professional help for them as parents, as well as for their child, although they do not necessarily expect miracles to happen as a result of this. These parents then tend to view the family's experience of CAMHS as helpful at first, but then as time goes on and their child's difficulties worsen, they conclude that it cannot have been helpful at all and consequently do not know where to turn next for further help for them and their child. Ultimately, these parents appear to be stuck in an unchanging situation or a problematic cycle.

Note. CAMHS = child and adolescent mental health services. From "The Journey Through and Beyond Mental Health Services in the United Kingdom: A Typology of Parents' Ways of Managing the Crisis of Their Teenage Child's Depression," by E. Stapley, M. Target, and N. Midgley, 2017, *Journal of Clinical Psychology, 73*(10), pp. 1433–1435 (https://doi.org/10.1002/jclp.22446). Copyright 2017 Wiley Periodicals, Inc. Reprinted with permission.

as described previously, the ideal-type description will include elements of other cases within the grouping as necessary to sufficiently describe that ideal type as a whole, as well as delineating the core features of the optimal case.

STEP 6: CHECKING CREDIBILITY

The credibility checks step in the ideal-type analysis process was originally formalized by Werbart and colleagues (Philips, Werbart, et al., 2007; Werbart et al., 2011, 2016). During this step, an independent researcher (ideally someone who has not been part of the analysis process so far) attempts to regroup the cases into the ideal types, using the ideal-type descriptions formed during the previous stage of the analysis (Philips, Werbart, et al., 2007; Werbart et al., 2011, 2016). Instances of disagreement should be discussed between the original and independent researcher until consensus can be reached, which could lead to refinements being made to the ideal types (Philips, Werbart, et al., 2007; Werbart et al., 2011, 2016). In our view, the aim of this step is not to establish whether the typology is objectively right or wrong. Rather, the aim of this step is to assess the clarity of the ideal types developed by the original researcher, through dialogue and consensus building with an independent researcher, including checking that the original researcher's interpretations are grounded in the data. In some cases, this may involve encouraging further reflection on any preconceived assumptions that the research team could have brought to their analysis.

This step can be carried out by providing an independent researcher with the descriptions of the ideal types and asking them to allocate each case to one of the ideal types, either by using the case reconstructions or the raw interview transcripts or data. Given the brevity of the case reconstructions, compared with the transcripts, use of the case reconstructions for this step would likely make it easier for an independent researcher to gain a sufficient grasp of the data set within a reasonably short time. Yet, an advantage of using the transcripts for this step is that they have not undergone any level of interpretation by the original researcher, whereas the case reconstructions were developed by the original researcher through their extraction of what they considered to be the relevant information from the transcripts. However, the latter approach is undoubtedly far more time intensive.

The credibility checks may (or may not) lead to cases being reassigned to different ideal-type clusters from those to which they had originally been assigned or to the refinement of the typology itself, the case reconstructions, or the ideal-type descriptions. For example, credibility checks could lead to the wording of the case reconstructions and the ideal-type descriptions being scrutinized and then rephrased as necessary to ensure that it is not ambiguous or confusing. The process of involving an independent researcher may be repeated several times, until the case reconstructions, typology, and/or ideal-type descriptions are sufficiently comprehensive and clear. Indeed, ideal-type analysis is a flexible, iterative process, and the researcher may revisit previous steps of the process throughout their analysis to refine and further develop the ideal types and case reconstructions as necessary (Werbárt et al., 2011, 2016). For an in-depth example of how credibility checks can be conducted in ideal-type analysis, also see the summary of the study conducted by O'Keeffe, Martin, Target, and Midgley (2019), provided in Chapter 6.

To aid discussions between the original researcher and the independent researcher, the level of agreement (i.e., in terms of to which ideal type each case reconstruction should be assigned) could be formally calculated as part of the credibility checking process. We see this as an optional stage in the process. For example, the percentage agreement could be calculated, and Cohen's kappa for pairwise comparisons could also be run (e.g., Stapley et al., 2017; Werbart et al., 2011, 2016). The rule of thumb is that a kappa statistic of .61 to .80 indicates substantial agreement between the original researcher and the independent researcher, whereas a kappa statistic of .21 to .40 would indicate only fair agreement (see Landis & Koch, 1977). Yet, the kappa statistic does have its limitations; for instance, the higher the number of categories (or ideal types), the more difficult it is to achieve a high kappa statistic (Brenner & Kliebsch, 1996). It is also important to remember that in our approach, we are not seeking to establish through this process whether the original researcher's typology is "correct"; rather, the aim is to highlight where there may be a potential need for further clarification and refinement of the typology.

In Stapley et al.'s (2017) ideal-type analysis of the experiences of parents of adolescents diagnosed with depression, the percentage agreement between the lead author and the independent researcher (who had no prior experience or knowledge of ideal-type analysis nor of working within the child mental health research field) was 75%. This meant that the independent researcher had designated seven of the 28 case reconstructions in this study as belonging to alternative ideal-type groupings to those to which they had originally been assigned by the lead author. The Cohen's kappa value was .62, which indicated substantial agreement between the lead author and the independent researcher. The discussions that followed this process ultimately did not lead to any case reconstructions being reassigned to a different ideal-type cluster from the one to which the lead author had originally assigned them. However, the discussions did lead to the wording of these seven case reconstructions and the ideal-type descriptions being scrutinized by the research team and the independent researcher to examine possible reasons why these discrepancies had occurred. Where the wording in the case reconstructions or the ideal-type descriptions was considered by the independent researcher to be ambiguous or confusing, it was then rephrased or expanded on accordingly by the research team.

Another method for providing credibility checks and refining one's typology could be through discussion of the typology with one's participant group or with the target group for whom the typology has been developed. For example, Griffiths et al. (2014) constructed a typology of the dynamics of living with a chronic illness from patients' perspectives, which was intended for clinicians to use in their clinical practice. As an additional stage in their analysis process, the authors held focus groups with patients and clinicians to discuss and refine their typology. This resulted in refinements being made to the names and descriptions of the types. The authors explained,

> Our prototype typology had included "Fearful waiting" and "Cautious optimism"; however, through discussion in the focus group, we clarified that both types were fearful of a return of distress, although people of the latter type were more hopeful than the former. These types were combined as "Past reminders." (Griffiths et al., 2014, p. 6)

STEP 7: MAKING COMPARISONS

In their write-up of the findings from their ideal-type analysis (described further in Chapter 4), we suggest that the researcher should include the ideal-type descriptions, a description of the optimal case for each ideal type, a summary of the similarities and differences between the cases within each type (compared with each other and with the optimal case), and a summary of the differences (and similarities) between the ideal types themselves. Through this process, the researcher bridges the gap between a focus on whole cases in their analysis, as well as on the patterns that exist between cases, which is a key feature of ideal-type analysis.

When describing the similarities and differences between the cases within each ideal type, the aim is to highlight to the reader why particular cases have all been assigned to a specific ideal type, while also capturing the inevitable variation in the experiences and perceptions of the cases within each of the ideal types. An example of how this looked for the "finding my own solutions" ideal type in Stapley et al.'s (2017) study can be seen in Exhibit 3.9. A description of the "finding my own solutions" ideal type and its optimal case can be seen in Exhibits 3.8 and 3.7, respectively. As described in Step 4, the designation of the optimal cases aids this process because the optimal cases are the orientation point to which the cases within each type can be compared.

To aid their description of the similarities and differences between the cases within the ideal types and between the ideal types themselves, the researcher could also use additional data collected about participants to make such comparisons. For instance, the researcher may have collected demographic, diagnostic, or clinical outcomes data as part of their study, and having constructed a typology, it may then be possible to compare cases within and between the types according to these data (e.g., Lindner et al., 2006; Philips, Werbart, et al., 2007; Stapley et al., 2017). This demonstrates the flexibility of the ideal-type analysis approach, which allows for the integration of quantitative data into the process of the comparison of cases within and between the types, which have been derived through qualitative methods.

EXHIBIT 3.9. Example of a Description of the Similarities and Differences Between the Six Cases Classified as the "Finding My Own Solutions" Ideal Type in Stapley et al.'s (2017) Study Compared With Each Other and With the Optimal Case

Like the optimal case, another parent within this ideal type feels that her daughter's difficulties have improved because of the new school to which she has moved her. In addition, this parent feels that although her daughter's therapy was not helpful in terms of alleviating her daughter's depression, perhaps it has still been "indirectly" helpful because it has given her daughter the attention she needed at that time. By contrast, the other four parents within this ideal type are particularly vociferous about their feelings of disappointment and anger in relation to the family's experience of CAMHS.

While the majority of the parents within this ideal type give examples of the types of solutions that they have found to help their child with their depression, outside of CAMHS, two of the parents within this ideal type do not give specific examples of these solutions. For instance, one of these parents states that he has no choice but to deal with his daughter's difficulties himself. However, unlike most of the other parents within this ideal type, he does not expand on his ideas for how he will do this, beyond suggesting potentially arranging therapy on a privately funded basis for his daughter.

Note. CAMHS = child and adolescent mental health services. From *Journey Through the Shadows: The Experience of Being the Parent of an Adolescent Diagnosed With Depression* (unpublished doctoral dissertation), by E. Stapley, 2016, University College London. Reprinted with permission.

For instance, following the development of their typology, Stapley et al. (2017) sought to explore the demographic differences between the three ideal types identified in their study, in terms of such factors as participants' employment status, marital status, and history of mental health issues. The authors found, for example, that a higher proportion of the "learning curve" parents were employed compared with the parents in the other two ideal types, and a lower proportion of the "learning curve" parents had a history of mental health issues. By contrast, a higher proportion of the "stuck" parents were unemployed and had a history of mental health issues. This additional step in their analysis helped inform the authors' reflections on the clinical implications of their typology. For instance, these findings suggested that the "stuck" parents might need help at the outset of their child's treatment from professionals at CAMHS to address difficulties in their home environments that could be affecting their capacity to manage their child's depression. No statistical significance testing of percentage differences was conducted in this study, given the small sample size, but one could test the statistical significance of the differences between the types, if such quantitative data were available, with a large enough sample size, and if such a test was relevant to the study's aim(s).

SUMMARY

Ideal-type analysis is described here as a predominantly inductive approach, whereby the ideal types are derived from the analysis in a bottom-up fashion, rather than being defined top-down beforehand. In our methodology, there are seven steps to conducting an ideal-type analysis: (a) becoming familiarized with the data set, (b) writing the case reconstructions, (c) constructing the ideal types, (d) identifying the optimal cases, (e) forming the ideal-type descriptions, (f) checking credibility, and (g) making comparisons. Ideal-type analysis is a flexible, iterative process, and the researcher may revisit steps multiple times throughout their analysis to refine and further develop their ideal types, case reconstructions, and interpretations as necessary over the course of the analysis (Werbart et al., 2011, 2016). A more detailed example of an ideal-type analysis study is provided in Chapter 6.

4

WRITING THE MANUSCRIPT

In this chapter, we explain how to write up an ideal-type analysis study, including the structure of the methodology and results sections, and ethical issues that should be considered. Also see Chapter 2 for a list of examples of published journal articles of studies using ideal-type analysis. We recommend following the American Psychological Association (APA) standards for reporting on qualitative research to ensure methodological integrity (Levitt et al., 2018). Throughout this chapter, we draw on Levitt et al.'s (2018) APA reporting standards, and we describe specifically what adhering to these standards may look like in the context of an ideal-type analysis.

WRITING THE INTRODUCTION

As with all qualitative studies, your introduction should

- introduce the research context for your study and the gap in existing knowledge that your study is addressing or the problem that your study is seeking to solve;

https://doi.org/10.1037/0000235-004
Essentials of Ideal-Type Analysis: A Qualitative Approach to Constructing Typologies,
by E. Stapley, S. O'Keeffe, and N. Midgley

- present a review of the literature relevant to your study; and

- state the purpose, aims, and objectives of your study, including the rationale for your study design: Why are you using a qualitative research design? Why are you specifically taking a typological approach?

Your introduction will then usually end by detailing the research question(s) that your study is aiming to address, with an overview of your epistemological position.

WRITING THE METHODOLOGY SECTION

The write-up must make the methodology transparent to the extent that it could be replicated by another researcher. Your methodology section will typically consist of several subsections, including descriptions of your participants, your approach to data collection and data analysis, and any ethical issues faced and how these have been addressed.

Participants

This subsection should contain a description of your participant group, including sample size, demographic characteristics (e.g., age, gender, ethnicity), your recruitment process (e.g., advertisements on social media, any incentives used), and your sampling strategy (e.g., purposive or convenience sampling).

Data Collection

This subsection should include a description of how you collected your data. For example, if you conducted semistructured interviews, then in this subsection, you would typically explain the following:

- what a semistructured interview is and what your rationale was for using this data collection technique,

- who collected the data (i.e., in terms of their role on the project) and what training they received,

- where the data collection took place (e.g., face to face or over the telephone, at participants' homes or elsewhere),

- the core questions or topics that were asked during the interviews,

- whether the interviews were audio recorded and transcribed (including whether the transcripts are verbatim representations of the audio files), and

- the range and mean length (plus standard deviation) of your interviews.

Data Analysis

Presenting a description of your data analysis process, in the context of an ideal-type analysis study, means detailing the steps to conducting an ideal-type analysis described in the previous chapter—not just listing them but describing briefly what you did in your study to carry out each step. For example, how did you familiarize yourself with your data set? What format did your case reconstructions take? How did you carry out your credibility checks on your ideal types, and how did you refine your analysis as a result? You should also specify what role your research team had, if applicable, throughout the data analysis process. Consideration could be given here to how the researchers' backgrounds and perspectives may have influenced the research process and how this was managed.

Ethical Considerations

Any research study requires the provision of detail on ethical considerations, including details about the ethical approval obtained for your study, the provision of informed consent by participants, and any steps taken to maintain participant confidentiality.

WRITING THE RESULTS SECTION

In an ideal-type analysis study, the results section will typically include

- the name and a description of each of your ideal types;

- the number of cases assigned to each ideal type;

- a description of the optimal case for each of your ideal types—this could be the case reconstruction for the optimal case, taking care not to compromise participant anonymity and confidentiality; and

- a summary of the key ways in which the cases assigned to each ideal type reflect that type (and how they may deviate from it), and the similarities and differences between these cases compared with each other and with the optimal case for each ideal type.

To summarize, the intention throughout your results section is to highlight to the reader what the ideal types are, how many cases have been assigned to each ideal type, why particular cases have been assigned to a specific ideal type, and the variation evident in the experiences and perceptions of the cases within each of the ideal types. Your results section could also include a table summarizing your ideal types (e.g., including the name, a brief description of each type, and the number of cases assigned to that type), as well as a table detailing the aggregated demographic characteristics for the cases assigned to each type. A summary of the key differences (and similarities) between the ideal types themselves should then be included in the discussion section of your write-up.

Quotations from interview or focus group transcripts or observation field notes, for example, or excerpts from case reconstructions should be included throughout your results section to illustrate or ground your inter-pretations in the data. Extracts from your data are used to augment your description of the findings from the analysis, not to replace it. You should take steps to guarantee the anonymity of participants and ensure that confidentiality is maintained. This can be achieved through removing or disguising any overtly identifying details within case reconstructions or source data before its inclusion in the write-up. Pseudonyms can also be used to disguise participants' identities. Nonetheless, there is still a distinct possibility that participants could recognize their own words in reports of the findings, even if no one else will. This means that you must be respectful and sensitive in how you report the findings of your study. For instance, in an ideal-type analysis, you should exercise sensitivity when naming and describing the types or groupings of participants you have derived from the data set. It is good practice to consider how your participant group would feel about the types, and the possibility of being classified as one of the types, should they read your write-up.

Consequently, it may be helpful to gather feedback from your participant group, or from individuals with similar experiences or demographics to your participant group, on the names and descriptions of your ideal types before publication. For instance, in a study of adolescents' experiences of risk and protective factors in relation to their mental health and well-being, three ideal types were derived from the data set: the adolescent with "multiple sources of support," the adolescent with "uncertain sources of support," and the adolescent with "self-initiated forms of support" (Eisenstadt, 2020; Eisenstadt et al., 2020). In initial drafts of the typology in Mia Eisenstadt's (2020) PhD research, the second ideal type was referred to as the adolescent "on shaky ground." However, before finalizing the names of the ideal types, the decision was made by Mia to consult a young person about the accessibility and acceptability of the names of the types, given that the types were intended to represent adolescents' experiences. After reading the names and descriptions of the types, the young person felt that the name "on shaky ground" had negative connotations for the prognosis of the young people within this grouping, which had, in fact, not been intended by Mia and her PhD advisors. Thus, instead, an alternative name—"uncertain sources of support"—was felt by both the young person and the research team to better capture the experiences of the participants within this type.

WRITING THE DISCUSSION SECTION

The discussion section of an ideal-type analysis study will typically include a summary of the ideal types, with descriptions and reflections on the key similarities and differences between the types. How the ideal types relate to, reflect, or deviate from existing findings in the literature relevant to your study must also be described. In addition, the discussion section should seek to highlight the novel contribution of your study to knowledge, detail the strengths and limitations of your study (including, for example, any limitations in terms of the transferability of your findings to other populations), make suggestions for future research, and provide insight into the implications of your findings, such as for policy or clinical practice.

SUMMARY

Levitt et al. (2018) outlined the APA standards for reporting on qualitative research, which offer a helpful framework to use to demonstrate methodological integrity. The results section in an ideal-type analysis study typically includes the name and a description of each of the ideal types, the number of cases assigned to each type, a description of the optimal case for each, and a summary of the within-type similarities and differences between cases. The discussion section then presents a summary of the ideal types, a comparison of the types with each other, and reflections on the significance of the findings.

5 VARIATIONS ON THE METHOD

In this chapter, we provide an overview of some of the different ways in which researchers have used ideal-type analysis in their studies. One of the features of qualitative research is that there is no one "right" way of doing things; rather, qualitative research design should be systematic yet responsive to the needs of a particular research study and the nature of the data available. Creativity is a key part of all good qualitative research—within a framework of methodological integrity and rigor.

A particular challenge for qualitative researchers, in general, is how to analyze data that may be complex and unwieldy (Vogl et al., 2018). Examples of complex data sets include longitudinal qualitative data, qualitative data drawn from multiple groups of participants, and data sets with multiple types of data, such as quantitative and qualitative data. Ideal-type analysis is one way of enabling researchers to make sense of a complex range of data because it allows different types of data to be integrated as part of the overall analytic approach.

https://doi.org/10.1037/0000235-005
Essentials of Ideal-Type Analysis: A Qualitative Approach to Constructing Typologies,
by E. Stapley, S. O'Keeffe, and N. Midgley

IDEAL-TYPE ANALYSIS WITH LONGITUDINAL QUALITATIVE DATA

Ideal-type analysis has frequently been applied to complex, longitudinal data sets, including research projects where participants have been interviewed twice or more across the duration of the project (e.g., Stapley et al., 2017; Werbart et al., 2011, 2016). These studies show how ideal-type analysis can be used flexibly, to allow researchers to use rich, longitudinal qualitative data sets to explore complex change processes over time. For example, as described in Chapter 3, Stapley et al. (2017) sought to explore parents' experiences of managing their teenage child's depression and engaging with mental health services over a 2-year period, drawing on interviews with parents at the point at which their child was referred for treatment at a specialist mental health service, then again after their child's treatment had ended, and once more, approximately 1 year later. Stapley et al. found three overarching types of parental experience from analyzing the interviews with the parents at all three points in their study using ideal-type analysis. The ideal types drew on the changing perceptions of help and experiences of living with their child's difficulties that the parents expressed over the course of the study. Thus, the longitudinal nature of the data was built into the ideal types.

Werbart and colleagues (2016, 2011) studied patterns of change over time in patients who have received psychotherapy. For instance, Werbart et al. (2016) examined changes in a clinical sample of young men's and women's self-representations across three times: pretherapy, the end of therapy, and 1.5 years later. However, unlike in Stapley et al.'s (2017) study, Werbart et al. (2016) analyzed each participant's data separately by time point and gender. In doing so, Werbart et al. (2016) found that most men's and women's descriptions of themselves changed over time, with cases being assigned to different ideal types at later times, compared with earlier times. For example, the number of women assigned to the "consolidated" ideal type, which included feeling content with oneself, had tripled at the end of therapy point, compared with at the pretherapy point.

As a further variation on the methodology, Werbart et al. (2016) also compared the self-representations of the clinical sample of young adult patients in their study with those of a nonclinical sample of young adults. The aim of this part of the study was to examine whether the changes observed over time in the clinical sample's descriptions of themselves may have simply been due to their growing maturity over the course of the study rather than due to the psychotherapy that they had received. The authors found that, unlike in the clinical sample, there were no changes over time in the quality of the young adults' descriptions of themselves in the nonclinical sample, whereas the descriptions given by the clinical sample became more reflective, detailed, and nuanced over time.

IDEAL-TYPE ANALYSIS WITH QUALITATIVE DATA FROM MULTIPLE GROUPS OF PARTICIPANTS

Researchers have also conducted ideal-type analysis with interviews from multiple groups of participants. For example, O'Keeffe, Martin, Target, and Midgley (2019) explored why young people with depression stopped going to therapy through separate interviews with the young people and their therapists. The case reconstructions in this ideal-type analysis study included the accounts of both the adolescent and therapist for each case. From their analysis of the case reconstructions, the authors identified three ideal types of adolescents who had prematurely stopped attending therapy: "dissatisfied" dropouts, "got-what-they-needed" dropouts, and "troubled" dropouts.

During their analysis, O'Keeffe, Martin, Target, and Midgley (2019) compared the two accounts (young person and therapist) within each case reconstruction to explore the extent to which their narratives were similar or different. They found that for the "got what they needed" and "troubled" dropouts in their study, there was a shared narrative between the young people and their therapists as to why the therapy had ended prematurely, whereas for the "dissatisfied" dropouts, the young people were highly critical of the therapy that they had received, but their therapists were typically unaware of the adolescents' criticisms of their treatment. However, the latter was not a hard-and-fast rule for the cases within this type; sometimes the therapists of the young people classified as this type did show some awareness of why the young person had stopped attending therapy. Overall, this study demonstrates how rich data from multiple perspectives can be integrated within case reconstructions to identify shared narratives and discrepancies and enable a phenomenon to be understood between different people—in this case, young people's reported perceptions of an event combined with the perceptions of professionals. See Chapter 6 for further details about this study (O'Keeffe, Martin, Target, & Midgley, 2019).

IDEAL-TYPE ANALYSIS WITH MULTIPLE TYPES OF DATA

Some studies using ideal-type analysis have employed multiple approaches to qualitative data collection, such as the use of in-depth interviews alongside observations. The data collected using these methods can then be integrated during the analysis process (e.g., Grytnes, 2011; Kettunen et al., 2018). Indeed, ideal-type analysis is concerned with the explanation of complex patterns of feelings and behaviors, and therefore, the use of multiple data sources may be informative in relation to the construction of typologies. For instance, Kettunen et al. (2018) constructed a typology of online shopping behavior drawing on multiple sources of qualitative data, including individual interviews, small-group discussions, and people's personal reflections, to gain a more complete picture of the phenomenon than perhaps could be obtained through the collection of just one type of data. For example, individual interviews might provide a better insight into personal motivations for online shopping behavior, whereas small-group discussions may illuminate people's differing experiences and opinions about this.

Researchers with a combination of both qualitative and quantitative data often come up against the challenge of how these different data types can be integrated (Lewin et al., 2009). Ideal-type analysis is a technique that is of relevance for mixed methods researchers and offers a possible approach for truly integrating qualitative and quantitative data (e.g., O'Keeffe, Martin, Target, & Midgley, 2019; Salomonsson & Sandell, 2011). For instance, in a randomized controlled trial of mother–infant psychoanalytic treatment for disturbances in the mother–infant relationship, Salomonsson and Sandell (2011) aimed to explore the associations between ideal types of mother–infant dyads and outcomes. The mothers completed outcome measures and took part in video recorded semistructured interviews, and the research team observed their interactions with their children. The ideal types were derived from the authors' analysis of the semistructured interviews. The authors found that mothers classified as the "participators" ideal type (who wanted to take an active role in therapeutic exploration) showed significant improvements in terms of their levels of sensitivity (as measured during observations of their interactions with their children) after receiving a mother–infant psychoanalytic intervention, whereas mothers classified as "abandoned" (who wanted to receive advice on how to handle their relationship with their child or partner) did not.

IDEAL-TYPE ANALYSIS AS THE SECOND STAGE OF QUALITATIVE DATA ANALYSIS

Some researchers have conducted an ideal-type analysis as the second stage in their qualitative data analysis process after first conducting a different type of analysis, such as interpretative phenomenological analysis

(Vachon et al., 2012) or a thematic analysis (Gisslevik et al., 2019; Kettunen et al., 2018). For example, in their study of how schoolchildren participated in and responded to education about sustainable food consumption, Gisslevik et al. (2019) initially conducted a thematic analysis of their data set (which included interviews with schoolchildren and observations of lessons), following Braun and Clarke's (2006) methodology for thematic analysis. This involved deriving cross-cutting themes from their data set to capture characteristics of the schoolchildren's participation in the lessons on sustainable food consumption, their behavior and expressions during the lessons, and their verbal and written contributions within the lessons. The authors then conducted an ideal-type analysis to synthesize and explore the relations between the themes to identify groups of pupils with similar characteristics or ways of participating in the lessons.

SUMMARY

The examples in this chapter indicate the diversity of research designs and data types that can be used for, and in conjunction with, ideal-type analysis. This includes longitudinal qualitative data, data from multiple groups of participants, data collected via multiple methods, and ideal-type analysis as the second stage in a broader qualitative data analysis process.

6 AN EXAMPLE OF AN IDEAL-TYPE ANALYSIS— FROM START TO FINISH

In this chapter, we describe a research study that used ideal-type analysis to offer a detailed example of the ideal-type analysis process. A more detailed report on the findings from this study has been published elsewhere (see O'Keeffe, Martin, Target, & Midgley, 2019), so this chapter focuses primarily on tracing the steps of the ideal-type analysis process used in this study from start to finish. This study was carried out by one of the authors of this volume (Sally O'Keeffe), under the supervision of another (Nick Midgley), as part of Sally's PhD research, in which she was investigating the concept of treatment dropout among a sample of adolescents who had all been diagnosed with depression and offered therapy. This chapter is a first-person account of Sally's study.

DEVELOPING MY RESEARCH QUESTION

Treatment dropout is defined as the premature ending of therapy when the client decides to end treatment without the agreement of their therapist (Warnick et al., 2012). Dropout is usually regarded as a negative way for

https://doi.org/10.1037/0000235-006
Essentials of Ideal-Type Analysis: A Qualitative Approach to Constructing Typologies,
by E. Stapley, S. O'Keeffe, and N. Midgley

therapy to conclude because it is assumed that a client must complete the full course of treatment to benefit from it (Cooper et al., 2018). In a previous study involving a sample of 406 adolescents who had received psychological treatment for depression, I sought to test this assumption (O'Keeffe, Martin, Goodyer, et al., 2019). Specifically, I tested the hypothesis that adolescents who had dropped out of treatment would have poorer clinical outcomes than adolescents who had completed treatment. Clinical outcomes were measured using a self-report questionnaire for depression severity, the Mood and Feelings Questionnaire (MFQ; Angold et al., 1987).

Contrary to what I had been expecting, there was no strong evidence for a difference in outcomes between adolescents who had completed treatment and those who had dropped out (O'Keeffe, Martin, Goodyer, et al., 2019). This surprising finding led me to question the meaning of the concept of dropout and the assumption that it is necessarily a bad thing in every case. Adolescents might drop out of therapy for different reasons, and not all of them would be associated with poor outcomes. Indeed, the majority of studies thus far have sought to describe those who drop out of therapy, but there is a dearth of knowledge about why adolescents do so (Ormhaug & Jensen, 2018). Thus, I was curious to examine why adolescents drop out of treatment and consider how this may refine how dropout is understood.

CONTEXT FOR THIS STUDY

This study was carried out in the context of a randomized controlled trial (RCT), the "Improving Mood With Psychoanalytic and Cognitive Therapies" study (IMPACT; Goodyer et al., 2011, 2017), which sought to investigate the efficacy of psychological therapies in the treatment of adolescent depression. The findings from the trial showed that the three interventions offered during the trial—cognitive behavior therapy, short-term psychoanalytic psychotherapy, and a brief psychosocial intervention—were equal in their clinical effectiveness, approximately 1 year after the end of treatment (Goodyer et al., 2017). The IMPACT trial was a multisite study across three regions in England, including London.

Alongside the IMPACT trial was its qualitative companion study, the "IMPACT-My Experience" study (IMPACT-ME; Midgley et al., 2014). In the IMPACT-ME study, qualitative interviews were carried out with adolescents, parents, and therapists taking part in the London region of the IMPACT trial. The IMPACT-ME study provided an important opportunity to learn from the perspectives of those involved in the trial and help make sense of the findings from the trial. The IMPACT-ME research team had already used some of the interview data to look at various issues, such as the kind of expectations that adolescents had about therapy before starting (Midgley et al., 2016), and now there was a chance to focus on the experience of those who had dropped out of therapy.

THE SAMPLE

Adolescents were invited to be interviewed three times as part of the IMPACT-ME study—before therapy, at the end of therapy, and then again 1 year later. Of the 127 adolescents who had taken part in the IMPACT trial in London, 102 had also taken part in at least one posttherapy interview as part of the IMPACT-ME study. Interviews had also been conducted with the therapists of 79 of these adolescents. For my study, I decided to purposively sample cases from this corpus who had been classified as having dropped out of treatment according to my established definition—the therapist's report that the ending of treatment was not mutually agreed. This provided a subsample of 32 adolescents who had dropped out of treatment, according to this definition, and who had completed at least one posttherapy interview about their experiences of therapy. For 26 of these adolescents, their therapist had also been interviewed separately about their perspective on the adolescent's therapy. Thus, because there were up to three interviews per case (up to two with the adolescent and one with their therapist), the data set in my study comprised 77 interviews for the 32 cases.

DATA COLLECTION

The interviews with participants in the IMPACT-ME study took place in a quiet and private space—usually a room at the mental health clinic where the adolescent had received their treatment or in their homes, depending on their preference. The interview schedules developed for the IMPACT-ME study were semistructured, allowing the researcher to guide the interview to cover the key topics of interest, while still enabling the conversation to be participant driven. The Experience of Therapy Interview outlined the key topics to explore in the interviews with the adolescents and therapists, including their expectations of therapy and their experiences of therapy (Midgley et al., 2011). Although the posttherapy interviews were designed to focus on the experience of therapy more generally, they always included some exploration of how and why therapy had ended, and the research team was encouraged to probe as fully as possible to explore the experience of those who had dropped out, given that this is a well-recognized issue in adolescent therapy (Eckshtain & Weisz, 2019). The interviews were intended to last approximately 60 minutes.

ETHICAL CONSIDERATIONS

A National Health Service research ethics committee granted ethical approval for the study. Fully informed written consent was sought from participants before their interviews were conducted (and for those participants under the age of 16 years, parental consent was also sought). However, consent is an ongoing process, and participants have the right to withdraw from the study at any point. This was explained to participants, and the research team was mindful throughout the conduct of the interviews to be sensitive to participants' needs. For instance, if a participant appeared upset or distressed during their interview, the researcher conducting the interview would ask the participant whether they were happy to continue with the interview or whether they would like to take a break.

Another important ethical consideration in this study related to confidentiality. While any information shared with the research team was confidential, it was important for the research team to acknowledge to participants, at the outset of their interviews, the limits to confidentiality. Researchers took the time to explain these limitations to participants—if the researcher became worried about the safety of the participant or someone else due to information disclosed during the interview, the researcher may have to speak to someone, such as their supervisor, about it.

An additional issue relating to confidentiality arose during the study, one we had not considered before the start of data collection. Because the therapists we interviewed were aware that we had also interviewed their clients and met with them since their treatment had ended, the therapists were often curious to know what their clients had told the researcher about their experience of therapy. This was particularly so for dropout cases when the therapists had often been left unclear about why their client had stopped coming to therapy, and they would sometimes ask the researcher conducting the interview how their client was. It was important that this information was not shared because we had made it clear to the adolescents that the information that they gave to the research team would not be shared with their therapists. We managed this by ensuring that the researcher who interviewed the adolescent's therapist had not interviewed the adolescent, thus avoiding the risk of them inadvertently sharing information about the adolescent with their therapist. In writing up the study, we were also careful not to include identifiable details that would allow the therapist to recognize their client or the adolescents to recognize particular things said by their therapists.

DECIDING HOW TO ANALYZE THE DATA

There was a range of qualitative methods that could have enabled me to explore the reasons for treatment dropout from the perspectives of the adolescents and their therapists. However, my sample was large for a qualitative study (32 cases consisting of 77 interviews) and was further complicated by having multiple perspectives (i.e., adolescent and therapist accounts) for most cases. Therefore, it was important to consider this when deciding how to analyze the data. Certain approaches, such as interpretative phenomenological analysis (Smith et al., 2009), usually require a small, homogenous sample, so they would not have been suitable for use with our data. However, an approach such as thematic analysis (Braun & Clarke, 2006) does not have this requirement and so would have allowed me to identify themes across the large sample of interviews in my study to examine reasons for treatment dropout from the perspectives of the adolescents and their therapists.

However, I decided that instead I wanted to use an approach that would allow me to identify whether there were more meaningful categories or "types" of treatment dropout than the existing definition of dropout implied. Therefore, I needed an approach to qualitative analysis that would enable me to identify clinically useful clusters of cases with similar (or different) experiences of treatment dropout. This was because if distinct types of treatment dropout could be identified, I felt it could then lead to reflection on and the development of clinical strategies for managing these different types of dropout. I discussed this with my PhD advisors, and we concluded that an approach such as thematic analysis would not be useful here, whereas ideal-type analysis could enable me to develop a typology of adolescents' experiences of treatment dropout.

Moreover, as my research was part of an RCT, a vast data set had been collected, and so in identifying types of treatment dropout using ideal-type analysis, it was anticipated that this approach could also facilitate the integration of the quantitative trial data with the qualitative data set, through comparing the characteristics and outcomes of adolescents with different experiences of treatment dropout. For instance, while my earlier study in my PhD research had found no strong evidence for adolescents who had dropped out of therapy having poorer clinical outcomes than those who had completed treatment (O'Keeffe, Martin, Goodyer, et al., 2019), the construction of a more refined categorization of dropout, using qualitative methods, would make it possible to explore whether there were differences in outcomes between different types of dropout.

DEFINING MY EPISTEMOLOGICAL POSITION

Because I did not have a background in philosophy and had originally been trained in quantitative research methods, I had never thought much about epistemology before doing a qualitative research project. At first, I found the readings on this topic difficult because they sometimes seemed abstract. However, I began to see that what I was being asked to do was to spell out, as explicitly as I could, how I understood the data that I had collected and was analyzing and whether I was seeing the language used by my participants as a "window" into their inner experiences or as something more interpreted or socially structured.

I came to see that I was approaching my analysis from a critical realist epistemological position. This position takes the view that researchers cannot have direct access to reality (Edgley et al., 2016). Consequently, I saw the interviews as providing an insight into participants' subjective perceptions of why they dropped out of therapy, but their reasons could not be viewed as an objective statement as to why such dropout occurred. Regardless of how forthcoming the participant was, the data could only tell us what the participant was willing to share, could remember, and was conscious of. Therefore, I considered that although there is a reality that underpins the phenomenon of therapy dropout, the perspectives included in this study could only provide an imperfect and partial impression of reality (Robinson & Smith, 2010).

I was aware that my analysis would be influenced by my knowledge, interests, and experiences, and that complete objectivity as a researcher was impossible. Therefore, throughout the data analysis process, I remained aware of my role in shaping and influencing the analysis (Madill et al., 2000). For instance, from my reading of the literature, I had begun my PhD research with assumptions that dropping out was a negative way for therapy to conclude and the result of something going wrong in treatment. Being consciously aware of these assumptions, keeping notes, and having discussions with others enabled me to remain open throughout the analysis to other possibilities about the meaning of dropout and reflect on any possible bias that I might have had toward or against particular explanations of dropout.

ANALYZING THE DATA

The steps for data analysis in my study, in general, followed those outlined in Chapter 3 of this volume. However, there were some differences in the approach—particularly in relation to Step 3, in terms of how I constructed the ideal types. While the steps outlined in Chapter 3 provide a structure for the researcher to use in conducting their ideal-type analysis, the steps should not be considered inflexible and can be adapted by the researcher, if necessary, according to the needs and nature of their study and data set.

Step 1: Becoming Familiarized With the Data Set

I had been involved in the wider research project that this study was part of, including conducting many of the interviews for the IMPACT-ME study, and I was therefore familiar with much of the data already. I transcribed some of the interviews myself, and the rest were transcribed with the help of other researchers in the team. This was not a small task, with each 1-hour interview typically taking 6 or 7 hours to transcribe. Once all the data had been transcribed, I listened to every interview in its entirety while reading the transcript. This was also a useful opportunity for me to correct any errors in the transcripts.

Step 2: Writing the Case Reconstructions

As described in Chapter 3, a case reconstruction is a written summary or description of the data for each participant. I wrote a case reconstruction (a one-page summary) for each case in the data set, incorporating both the adolescent and therapist perspectives. This involved reading the adolescent and therapist interview transcripts several times and listing all the elements from the transcripts that related to three predetermined domains that were of interest in relation to my research question: how the adolescent came to be referred for therapy, their experience of therapy, and how therapy ended. Exhibit 6.1 shows two example case reconstructions from my study, presented in brief to maintain participant confidentiality. Participants have also been given pseudonyms to protect their identities.

EXHIBIT 6.1. Two Example Case Reconstructions Written for the O'Keeffe, Martin, Target, and Midgley (2019) Study of Adolescent Treatment Dropout

Craig[a]

Adolescent's Perspective

Domain 1: Referral

Adolescent reported being referred to CAMHS because he was feeling down and had become socially withdrawn.

Domain 2: Story of Therapy

Adolescent described not finding therapy helpful. He reported feeling that the therapist did not listen to him or care about him because they would forget the things he had said in the previous session, and the therapist would end the sessions early. He reported that he did not have the energy for therapy because it was not benefiting him.

Domain 3: Therapy Ending

Adolescent reported stopping therapy because he felt it was pointless and tiring, and he was frustrated with the therapist focusing on topics he did not think were relevant to his difficulties.

Therapist's Perspective

Domain 1: Referral

The therapist reported that the young person was socially withdrawn.

Domain 2: Story of Therapy

The therapist reported that it had become apparent at the start of treatment that the adolescent was skeptical and cynical about therapy. The therapist described how the adolescent would sometimes engage well in the therapy, while at other times, the adolescent seemed to think that it was a waste of time and would reject it.

Domain 3: Therapy Ending

The therapist described how the adolescent had started missing sessions and then had stopped attending the sessions entirely. Therapy ended when the adolescent's mom phoned to say that he did not want to return. However, the therapist described feeling that the adolescent could not face coming back because he was reaching the point of starting to make use of the therapy, and he was beginning to open up to the therapist. The therapist also described feeling that the adolescent had felt afraid about becoming dependent on them, so he had decided to stop coming. The therapist viewed this as a wasted opportunity and felt disappointed by the premature ending of treatment.

Sky

Adolescent's Perspective

Domain 1: Referral

Adolescent reported being depressed, moody, and stressed.

Domain 2: Story of Therapy

Adolescent described finding it helpful to share her problems with her therapist and that it helped her see things in a more positive way. She also reported some negative aspects of therapy—she found the therapist inflexible and found it difficult to challenge things that she disagreed with.

(continues)

EXHIBIT 6.1. Two Example Case Reconstructions Written for the O'Keeffe, Martin, Target, and Midgley (2019) Study of Adolescent Treatment Dropout (*Continued*)

Domain 3: Therapy Ending

Sky reported stopping therapy because she had got the help that she needed and did not see a need to keep going.

Therapist's Perspective

Domain 1: Referral

The therapist reported that the adolescent was referred with depression and anger problems.

Domain 2: Story of Therapy

The therapist reported that in the sessions, they focused on challenging the adolescent's unhelpful thought patterns. The therapist reported that this appeared to have been helpful for the adolescent, who seemed to be committed to the therapy.

Domain 3: Therapy Ending

The therapist reported feeling puzzled about why the adolescent had stopped coming to therapy. She seemed frustrated that she did not understand why the therapy had ended in this way because she felt that they had worked well together. The therapist described a wish to understand why the adolescent had stopped attending therapy.

Note. CAMHS = child and adolescent mental health services. From "'I Just Stopped Going': A Mixed Methods Investigation Into Types of Therapy Dropout in Adolescents With Depression," by S. O'Keeffe, P. Martin, M. Target, and N. Midgley, 2019, *Frontiers in Psychology, 10*, p. 75 (https://doi.org/10.3389/fpsyg.2019.00075). Copyright 2019 by Frontiers in Psychology. Reprinted with permission.
[a]Names have been changed to preserve the anonymity of the individuals involved.

Step 3: Constructing the Ideal Types

The process of organizing the cases into ideal types or clusters of similar cases can be conducted using the entire data set from the outset. However, in this study, given my relatively large sample, I took a different approach. The ideal types were initially constructed in my study using half of the data set (i.e., 16 of the 32 cases). By constructing the initial typology using 16 cases, I was then able to test whether 16 different cases (i.e., the other half of the data set) could be classified into these types. If the initial typology could be used to classify the second half of the data set, then this would support the typology as being comprehensive and robust, whereas if it were not possible to classify all these cases, it could lead to the refinement of some of the types or the addition of new types. Because I was undertaking the analysis independently, I also decided to include initial credibility checks at this stage by independent researchers, to ensure that my analysis was grounded in the data. Therefore, in my study, Step 3 consisted of three substages: (a) constructing the initial typology, (b) conducting initial credibility checks, and (c) testing the remaining cases in the data set.

Constructing the Initial Typology

To construct the initial typology, for which I used the first half of the data set ($n = 16$), I systematically compared each case with all the other 15 cases. I was looking for similarities and differences in participants' explanations and reasons for stopping therapy and then grouping together the case reconstructions that seemed to portray similar explanations and reasons. I found that working with printed copies of the case reconstructions was the most productive way for me to do this because it allowed me to annotate and color code the case reconstructions in terms of the similarities I was finding between cases, and then I could physically group similar cases together. This made it easy to experiment with different ways of clustering the cases, by physically moving them and then seeing how they fitted together until I had found what seemed like the best fit for the data set in terms of the clusters of cases. By best fit, I mean that the cases within each cluster were as homogenous as possible, and the ideal types or clusters were clearly distinct.

To aid with the case comparison process, I initially looked for evidence of highly different experiences between cases, such as the two cases shown in Exhibit 6.1. Craig was someone who had been highly dissatisfied with his therapy, in contrast to the second case, Sky, who reported a mostly positive experience of therapy. These individuals clearly had very different reasons for stopping treatment and could be used as yardsticks to compare them with other cases in the data set. Accordingly, I was then able to consider for each subsequent case whether it was more like Craig, Sky, or neither. Was there something distinctive about the case that was not captured in my current clusters of cases? This aided the case comparison process. The case comparison process ultimately led to the construction of four ideal types, outlined in Exhibit 6.2. These were the "improved" dropout, the "dissatisfied" dropout, the "rupture" dropout, and the "troubled" dropout. Craig and Sky, as presented in Exhibit 6.1, represent the "dissatisfied" and "improved" dropout types, respectively.

Because each case should only belong to one ideal type, a challenge was how to deal with "borderline cases"—when it was not clear which ideal type or cluster a case should be part of. For example, I had identified a "dissatisfied" dropout type—in which adolescents stopped attending therapy because they were not satisfied with their treatment and did not find it helpful—and an "improved" dropout type—in which adolescents were largely satisfied with their experience of therapy but stopped going because they

EXHIBIT 6.2. Initial Typology Developed in the O'Keeffe, Martin, Target, and Midgley (2019) Study of Adolescent Treatment Dropout

Type	Summary	Necessary conditions
1. The "improved" dropout	Adolescent stopped attending therapy because they felt better.	Adolescent reported not seeing a need to keep going to therapy because they felt better or it was due to end soon.
		Adolescent attributed positive change, to some extent, to the therapy.
		Therapist did not appear to be worried about adolescent stopping therapy.
2. The "dissatisfied" dropout	Adolescent stopped attending therapy because it failed to meet their needs.	Adolescent reported stopping therapy because they did not find it helpful.
		Adolescent was critical of the therapy that they received.
		Therapist recognized adolescent's difficulty attending or engaging in the sessions.
3. The "rupture" dropout	Adolescent stopped attending therapy because of a breakdown in the therapeutic relationship.	Adolescent reported losing trust in their therapist because of a specific event in the therapy.
		Adolescent was critical of the therapy they received and suggested that it would put them off seeking therapy again in the future.
		Therapist was unsure why the adolescent had suddenly stopped attending their sessions.
4. The "troubled" dropout	Adolescent stopped attending therapy because it was not the right time for them to engage in therapy.	Adolescent presented with complex difficulties (e.g., homelessness, history of abuse).
		Adolescent linked stopping therapy to external difficulties.
		Therapist felt that the adolescent could not have engaged in any type of therapy at that time because of the lack of stability in their life.

Note. A case must meet all necessary conditions to be coded as that type. From "'I Just Stopped Going': A Mixed Methods Investigation Into Types of Therapy Dropout in Adolescents With Depression," by S. O'Keeffe, P. Martin, M. Target, and N. Midgley, 2019, *Frontiers in Psychology*, *10*, p. 75 (https://doi.org/10.3389/fpsyg.2019.00075). Copyright 2019 by Frontiers in Psychology. Reprinted with permission.

felt they had taken from therapy what they needed. While these dropout types sound clearly distinct, some cases shared characteristics of both types. For instance, some cases generally reflected the "improved" dropout type, yet they were critical about aspects of their therapy (which reflected the "dissatisfied" dropout type). I discussed this dilemma with my PhD advisors, who helped me to see that despite having some criticisms of their therapy, the "improved" dropouts did not report this as being their reason for stopping therapy, and thus their dissatisfaction appeared to have less weight in their decision to end treatment, compared with the "dissatisfied" dropouts. Recognizing this distinction led me to clarify what the core elements of each of these ideal types (and those of the others) were and which elements could be variable across cases when determining to which ideal type each case belonged.

Consequently, I developed specific criteria or "necessary conditions" that each case assigned to each ideal type had to fulfill to be assigned to that particular type, to make my decisions about case classifications more transparent. I recorded these specific criteria in a table detailing my typology (see Exhibit 6.2). The development of this table, comprising the necessary conditions for a case to fit within a specific ideal type, provided an audit trail and enabled me to take a systematic and rigorous approach to my data analysis.

Conducting Initial Credibility Checks

Because I had independently prepared the case reconstructions and formed the initial ideal types, I felt at this point that it was important to get substantial feedback on the ideal types and the extent to which they were intuitive to classify cases to before proceeding further with my analysis. Therefore, I carried out credibility checks to assess whether the definition of each ideal type was sufficiently clear and whether independent researchers could reliably classify cases into the types that I had constructed. To do this, two independent researchers used the table in Exhibit 6.2 to each recategorize six cases from my initial sample. Thus, a total of 12 cases from the first half of the data set were used in this process (selected to ensure representation of cases across all four types). My intention was to use this process to adapt or refine the typology as necessary at this point.

The independent researchers were provided with the interview transcripts for each case and were asked to tick the necessary conditions in the table that were met for that case and then select the type they felt the case should be categorized as. Once the ratings were complete, I assessed the degree of agreement between the independent researchers and myself. This was based on (a) the percentage agreement between the independent researchers and myself, in terms of the classification of cases into the ideal types and (b) an assessment of the degree of similarity between the researchers in their ratings of the presence or absence of each of the necessary conditions for each ideal type for each case, using Gower distance (Gower, 1971). Gower distance is calculated from a similarity matrix, in which each characteristic for each participant is coded 0 (*coders do not agree*) or 1 (*coders agree*). Gower distance is the number of categories that both raters have rated as present, divided by the number of categories that one or both raters rated as present. Values range between 0 (*no similarity*) and 1 (*perfect similarity*).

The first rater was a qualitative postdoctoral researcher who had experience of ideal-type analysis. Good agreement (83%) for assigning the cases to the types was established, with disagreement on one of the cases. Agreement was also good for the necessary conditions (Gower distance = .83). A second rater then coded a further six cases. The second rater was a postgraduate researcher, without experience of ideal-type analysis. There was 100% agreement on the types, and agreement on the necessary conditions was good (Gower distance = .78). During this process, the researchers were given the option to select an "Other" type, to allow for the possibility that the typology may not have been comprehensive enough for the cases. However, both co-raters reported that the typology had been comprehensive enough for the cases they had coded and did not code any cases to the Other category.

Following discussions with the independent researchers and my PhD advisors, we came to question the distinction between the "dissatisfied" and "rupture" types. Given that the one case currently assigned to the "rupture" type was dissatisfied with their treatment as a result of a rupture in the relationship with their therapist, the question arose of whether the rupture case could, in fact, better be understood as one example of the "dissatisfied" type, rather than as a separate type. Therefore, the decision was made to merge the "rupture" dropout type with the "dissatisfied" dropout type, with the understanding that the "rupture" type represented variation in how dissatisfaction may occur during treatment (e.g., as the result of a specific incident), rather than representing a different type of dropout altogether. Another question raised during this process was about the name of the "improved" dropout type. The word "improved" seemed to imply clinical change, but the types were based on subjective experiences rather than clinical change (although clinical change was something that I was later interested in exploring). Thus, I decided to rename the "improved" dropout type to the "got-what-they-needed" type to reflect better the subjective experience of feeling ready to stop therapy, rather than implying objective clinical change.

The changes to my typology described here reflect how one might adapt the ideal types during the analysis to reach a state of best fit for the data set. This may include renaming ideal types, merging ideal types, and better defining the criteria by which cases are classified into ideal types. The researcher should remain open to feedback and the ideas of others to ensure that their typology is intuitive and a good fit for the data. The revised (and final) typology in my study, as a result of this process, consisted of three dropout types (shown in Exhibit 6.3).

EXHIBIT 6.3. Final Typology Developed in the O'Keeffe, Martin, Target, and Midgley (2019) Study of Adolescent Treatment Dropout

Type	Summary	Necessary conditions
1. "Dissatisfied" dropout	Adolescent reported stopping attending therapy because it failed to meet their needs.	Adolescent reported stopping therapy because they did not find it helpful. Adolescent was critical of the therapy they received. Therapist reported that adolescent had difficulty attending or engaging in the sessions.
2. "Got-what-they-needed" dropout	Adolescent reported stopping attending therapy because they felt better.	Adolescent reported not seeing a need to keep going to therapy because they felt better or it was due to end soon. Adolescent attributed positive change, to some extent, to the therapy. Therapist did not appear to be worried about the adolescent stopping therapy.
3. "Troubled" dropout	Adolescent reported stopping attending therapy because they felt that it was not the right time for them to engage in therapy.	Adolescent presented with complex difficulties (e.g., homelessness, history of abuse). Adolescent linked (or implied) their reasons for stopping therapy as being due to their external difficulties. Therapist suggested that the adolescent could not have engaged in any type of therapy at that time because of the lack of stability in their life.

Note. From "'I Just Stopped Going': A Mixed Methods Investigation Into Types of Therapy Dropout in Adolescents With Depression," by S. O'Keeffe, P. Martin, M. Target, and N. Midgley, 2019, *Frontiers in Psychology, 10,* p. 75 (https://doi.org/10.3389/fpsyg.2019.00075). Copyright 2019 by Frontiers in Psychology. Reprinted with permission.

Testing the Remaining Cases in the Data Set

The final typology, as shown in Exhibit 6.3, was then used to assess the remaining cases in the data set ($n = 16$) to see whether the three ideal types could account for all the remaining cases in the data set. This acted as a test of the types' validity—whether these three types reflected all the cases in the data set. I carried out the assessment of the remaining data set myself (although further credibility checks were also carried out again later, as described next). The three types proved to be sufficient to classify the second half of the data set also, although some refinement of the descriptions of each type was needed to capture the key features of the experiences of all the cases assigned to each type.

My study shows how a researcher can use ideal-type analysis to initially conduct a data-driven inductive analysis on part of a data set and then move toward testing the typology deductively on the rest of the data set to assess its relevance and comprehensiveness. During this process, it may be necessary to develop additional ideal-type clusters or to go back and revise and modify the original types, and the researcher must be open to this possibility throughout the analysis.

Step 4: Identifying the Optimal Cases

Having formed the ideal types, I sought to identify an optimal case for each of the three types. The aim of this step is to identify the case that best represents or illustrates each cluster of similar cases. To do this, I compared each of the case reconstructions within each cluster, contrasting each case with every other case in that cluster, and identified the case that best characterized the necessary conditions (as shown in Exhibit 6.3) for that ideal type.

Step 5: Forming the Ideal-Type Descriptions

Having established the three ideal types and identified an optimal case for each, I then sought to form a detailed description of each of the ideal types. To do this, the optimal cases were used as orientation points for comparing the other cases to identify the salient features of each type. As shown in Exhibit 6.3, the three types of dropout were the "dissatisfied" dropout, the "got-what-they-needed" dropout, and the "troubled" dropout. The full descriptions of the ideal types outlined the necessary conditions each case assigned to each type had to fulfill.

Step 6: Conducting Additional Credibility Checks

Given the refinements I had made to the typology following the first round of credibility checks, I decided to also ask another independent researcher (who had not been involved in the previous credibility checks) to recategorize the entire data set using the final version of the typology shown in Exhibit 6.3. This independent researcher was a postgraduate researcher without experience of ideal-type analysis. Agreement between the independent researcher and myself was excellent, with agreement on 96% of the cases with respect to the types that they were classified as, and there was also good agreement on the necessary conditions (Gower distance = .71). As described in Chapter 3, the purpose of this step was not to establish the extent to which my typology was "correct," but rather to ensure that my interpretations were grounded in and clearly reflective of the data—which I had confidence in after reaching a good level of agreement with the independent researcher.

Step 7: Making Comparisons

As this study drew on the perspectives of both adolescents and their therapists, I paid close attention to the extent to which the account of the adolescent and therapist for each case was similar or different and ensured that this was reported in the write-up of my results. For instance, I found that for "dissatisfied" dropouts, the young people were highly critical of the therapy they had received, but their therapists were often unaware of the adolescents' criticisms of their treatment. In contrast, in the other dropout types, there was more of a shared narrative between the young people and their therapists—there tended to be overlap in their accounts of why the therapy had ended.

I also began to develop hypotheses about the dropout types. Because the cases were participants in an RCT, a wealth of data had been collected over a 2-year period, allowing me to test these hypotheses. For example, as described earlier in this chapter, clinical impairment and outcomes were measured using the MFQ, which participants completed before starting treatment and then at five follow-up assessments, including at the end of treatment and 1 year later. Examples of the subsequent hypotheses that were tested are described here briefly, but for full details of the empirical studies, please see the published article (O'Keeffe, Martin, Target, & Midgley, 2019). Statistical analyses were conducted using mixed-effects models to test these hypotheses.

Hypothesis 1: "Got-What-They-Needed" Dropouts Were Less Impaired at Baseline Compared With "Dissatisfied" Dropouts

Given that the "got-what-they-needed" dropouts reported stopping therapy because they felt they had benefited from it, I hypothesized that they were less impaired before starting therapy and thus required a short treatment to feel sufficiently improved to stop treatment. However, statistical analyses did not support Hypothesis 1 because there was no evidence that "got-what-they-needed" dropouts were less impaired in depression severity at baseline than the "dissatisfied" dropouts. This suggested that the differences between these two groups were perhaps more related to what had occurred in therapy than to the level of impairment with which the adolescents had entered therapy.

Hypothesis 2: "Got-What-They-Needed" Dropouts Will Have Better Long-Term Clinical Outcomes Compared With "Dissatisfied" Dropouts

Given that the "got-what-they-needed" dropouts reported stopping therapy having felt sufficiently improved, whereas "dissatisfied" dropouts reported having stopped therapy due to not finding it helpful, I hypothesized that the "got-what-they-needed" dropouts would have better clinical outcomes compared with the "dissatisfied" dropouts. Essentially, I was interested in whether adolescents' reported perceptions of whether they felt that their therapy had helped corresponded with their clinical outcomes. Statistical analyses showed some support for Hypothesis 2 because "got-what-they-needed" dropouts had better observed outcomes at each point compared with "dissatisfied" dropouts, and this difference was significant at the 36-week (after baseline or pretherapy) follow-up point. However, this difference was not statistically significant at later points (52 and 86 weeks).

WRITING THE MANUSCRIPT

The descriptions of the ideal types were presented in the manuscript, followed by a summary of the optimal case for each type. The optimal case for each type provided a detailed example, which illustrated that ideal type in its most pure form. A pseudonym was assigned for each optimal case, and identifying details were changed or removed throughout the manuscript to maintain participant anonymity and confidentiality. Where there was notable variation in participants' experiences within a type, this was also reported, with quotations and reference to the content of the case reconstructions that showed this. The hypotheses and results from the analyses with additional data were also presented. To read the full report of this study, see the published paper (O'Keeffe, Martin, Target, & Midgley, 2019).

SUMMARY

This chapter described an example of conducting an ideal-type analysis from start to finish. The study presented shows how the methodology for conducting ideal-type analysis can be flexed and adapted depending on the needs of the study. It also shows how ideal-type analysis can facilitate mixed-methods research. Ideal-type analysis was used in this study to construct a typology comprising three distinct categories of the reasons for treatment dropout from the perspectives of both adolescents and their therapists. Seeking to deconstruct the meaning of dropout led to the development of a new concept for the research literature in this area: types of dropout.

7 SUMMARY AND CONCLUSIONS

Ideal-type analysis has its roots in the thinking and methodology of sociologists Max Weber (1904) and Uta Gerhardt (1994). Gerhardt's methodology for ideal-type analysis was originally developed as a qualitative sociology research method but has since been applied to qualitative psychology research. Ideal-type analysis is a flexible method with respect to the data that can be collected, and its use (and the type of data collected) ultimately depends on the research aims of any given study. "How," "why," and "what" research questions are all appropriate for ideal-type analysis. Although a single researcher can carry out an ideal-type analysis, the approach benefits enormously from having a team involved (McLeod, 2011).

In our methodology, there are seven steps to conducting an ideal-type analysis: (a) becoming familiarized with the data set, (b) writing the case reconstructions, (c) constructing the ideal types, (d) identifying the optimal cases, (e) forming the ideal-type descriptions, (f) checking credibility, and (g) making comparisons. Ideal-type analysis is a flexible, iterative process, and the researcher may revisit steps multiple times throughout their analysis to refine and further develop their ideal types, case reconstructions,

https://doi.org/10.1037/0000235-007
Essentials of Ideal-Type Analysis: A Qualitative Approach to Constructing Typologies,
by E. Stapley, S. O'Keeffe, and N. Midgley

and interpretations as necessary over the course of the analysis (Werbart et al., 2011, 2016). Moreover, the steps to conducting an ideal-type analysis should not be considered inflexible but can be adapted by the researcher if necessary, according to the needs and nature of their study and data set.

BENEFITS AND ADVANTAGES OF THE METHOD

Despite the utility and prominence of typologies within psychology, there is, in fact, little methodological guidance available to explain the process of constructing a typology, particularly as a qualitative method for analyzing data (Kluge, 2000). Ideal-type analysis is an important addition to the family of qualitative research methods because it offers a systematic, rigorous methodological approach to such analysis (Gerhardt, 1994).

Each type, or grouping of participants, in an ideal-type analysis, is formed through the systematic comparison of individual participants with each other. In this way, ideal-type analysis provides a means for the researcher to focus on the individual participant's experience, as well as on the patterns that exist across the data set and within and between groups in the data set (Werbart et al., 2016).

The types formed through ideal-type analysis can be considered hypotheses about aspects of human behavior, experience, or perception, which are intended to be tested against and, in doing so, enhance our understanding of reality or a given psychological phenomenon (Lindner, 2006; Stuhr & Wachholz, 2001; Wachholz & Stuhr, 1999). This means that as new typologies are formed, new hypotheses are created about how a particular psychological phenomenon can be understood. Consequently, typologies provide the potential to generalize beyond the sample under study (Williams, 2002).

Ideal-type analysis is a flexible method that can be used with a diverse range of qualitative data sources, including interview or focus group transcripts, observations, field notes, diaries, clinical case notes, and other sources of textual or visual data. Ideal-type analysis has also been used in conjunction with and to make sense of complex data sets, including longitudinal qualitative data, data from multiple groups of participants, and data collected via multiple methods, including integrating qualitative and quantitative data sources in the analysis process.

LIMITATIONS OF THE METHOD

Ideal-type analysis is not without its limitations. It shares many of its limitations with other inductive approaches to qualitative data analysis because the types identified in a given study may not be the only types of behavior, opinion, or experience that could be identified in relation to a particular construct, and other types may be found in other samples and settings. For example, in their ideal-type analysis of parents' experiences of managing their teenage child's depression and engaging with mental health services over a 2-year period, Stapley et al. (2017) questioned whether the three ideal types found in their study would transfer or extend, for instance, to those parents who were uncontactable or who chose not to be interviewed by the research team at the follow-up points of the study. The possibility that additional ideal types could be identified in relation to the same construct with a larger sample or a different sample cannot be ruled out.

A typology, in an ideal-type analysis, is constructed from the point of view of the researcher developing it. It cannot be said with certainty whether another researcher will construct the same types. This reflects a critical realist and constructivist epistemological perspective, which we propose readily cohere with the ideal-type analysis method. Therefore, in general, we would argue that, rather than trying to preclude such subjectivity or undermine its utility, what is important instead, to enhance the trustworthiness of the research, is that the researcher consciously and reflexively examines any potential biases or assumptions that they could bring to the research, including being transparent to the reader about what these are and the potential influence of these on the research. The trustworthiness of the research, such as the degree to which the analysis is grounded within and reflects the data, can also be enhanced by using an established qualitative analysis method with a systematic procedure (as we have outlined in this volume), taking a team approach to analysis, and inviting independent researchers to conduct credibility checks on the analysis. The aim of the latter in our approach to ideal-type analysis is to provoke discussion and refinement during the analysis process, not to determine the degree to which the typology is "correct."

In the initial stages of ideal-type analysis, when large amounts of in-depth interview data are condensed into comparatively brief case reconstructions summarizing the relevant content of each interview, arguably, this may result in the loss of the more minute details in participants' interviews (Stapley et al., 2017). Indeed, reflecting on their study of the changes in young adult psychotherapy patients' representations of their mothers and fathers over time, Werbart et al. (2011) acknowledged that while ideal-type analysis had allowed them to capture changes in the content of the young adults' descriptions over time, more nuanced changes in the language and structure of the descriptions were lost in the analysis process. Thus, the authors concluded that ideal-type analysis was "too coarse a method for studying such patterns" (Werbart et al., 2011, p. 112). However, perhaps structuring participants' case reconstructions specifically around the language and structure of their descriptions, rather than solely focusing on content, might facilitate such an analysis taking place.

CONCLUSIONS

We propose that ideal-type analysis, as a qualitative data analysis technique, offers a way of studying the psychological world that has great value. Ideal-type analysis offers something different to thematic approaches to qualitative research or to ethnographic or case study research methods, in that it provides a rigorous, step-by-step methodology for researchers to use specifically to develop typologies from qualitative data. In this way, ideal-type analysis enables the qualitative researcher to focus on the experiences and perspectives of whole cases, as well as on the patterns arising across the data set, through rich descriptions of groups of participants and exploration of the similarities and differences between their experiences and perspectives.

References

Ainsworth, M. D., & Bell, S. M. (1970). Attachment, exploration, and separation: Illustrated by the behavior of one-year-olds in a strange situation. *Child Development, 41*(1), 49–67. https://doi.org/10.2307/1127388

Aldridge, A. A., & Roesch, S. C. (2008). Developing coping typologies of minority adolescents: A latent profile analysis. *Journal of Adolescence, 31*(4), 499–517. https://doi.org/10.1016/j.adolescence.2007.08.005

Angold, A., Costello, E. J., Pickles, A., & Winder, F. (1987). *The development of a questionnaire for use in epidemiological studies in children and adolescents.* MRC Child Psychiatry Research Unit.

Armstrong, D., Gosling, A., Weinman, J., & Marteau, T. (1997). The place of inter-rater reliability in qualitative research: An empirical study. *Sociology, 31*(3), 597–606. https://doi.org/10.1177/0038038597031003015

Ayres, L., Kavanaugh, K., & Knafl, K. A. (2003). Within-case and across-case approaches to qualitative data analysis. *Qualitative Health Research, 13*(6), 871–883. https://doi.org/10.1177/1049732303013006008

Baumrind, D. (1991). The influence of parenting style on adolescent competence and substance use. *The Journal of Early Adolescence, 11*(1), 56–95. https://doi.org/10.1177/0272431691111004

Bengtsson, B., & Hertting, N. (2014). Generalization by mechanism: Thin rationality and ideal-type analysis in case study research. *Philosophy of the Social Sciences, 44*(6), 707–732. https://doi.org/10.1177/0048393113506495

Bohane, L., Maguire, N., & Richardson, T. (2017). Resilients, overcontrollers and undercontrollers: A systematic review of the utility of a personality typology method in understanding adult mental health problems. *Clinical Psychology Review, 57*(July), 75–92. https://doi.org/10.1016/j.cpr.2017.07.005

Bramley, N., & Eatough, V. (2005). The experience of living with Parkinson's disease: An interpretative phenomenological analysis case study. *Psychology & Health, 20*(2), 223–235. https://doi.org/10.1080/08870440412331296053

Braun, V., & Clarke, V. (2006). Using thematic analysis in psychology. *Qualitative Research in Psychology, 3*(2), 77–101. https://doi.org/10.1191/1478088706qp063oa

Brenner, H., & Kliebsch, U. (1996). Dependence of weighted kappa coefficients on the number of categories. *Epidemiology, 7*(2), 199–202. https://doi.org/10.1097/00001648-199603000-00016

Burgess, R. G. (1984). *In the field: An introduction to field research.* Routledge.

Busse, A. (2005). Individual ways of dealing with the context of realistic tasks—first steps towards a typology. *ZDM, 37*(5), 354–360. https://doi.org/10.1007/s11858-005-0023-3

Byrne, M. (2001). The concept of informed consent in qualitative research. *AORN Journal, 74*(3), 401–403. https://doi.org/10.1016/S0001-2092(06)61798-5

Charmaz, K. (2006). *Constructing grounded theory: A practical guide through qualitative analysis.* SAGE.

Charmaz, K. (2017). The power of constructivist grounded theory for critical inquiry. *Qualitative Inquiry, 23*(1), 34–45. https://doi.org/10.1177/1077800416657105

Charmaz, K., & Henwood, K. (2017). Grounded theory. In C. Willig (Ed.), *The SAGE handbook of qualitative research in Psychology* (pp. 238–256). SAGE. https://doi.org/10.4135/9781526405555

Clatworthy, J., Buick, D., Hankins, M., Weinman, J., & Horne, R. (2005). The use and reporting of cluster analysis in health psychology: A review. *British Journal of Health Psychology, 10*(3), 329–358. https://doi.org/10.1348/135910705X25697

Cooper, A. A., Kline, A. C., Baier, A. L., & Feeny, N. C. (2018). Rethinking research on prediction and prevention of psychotherapy dropout: A mechanism-oriented approach. *Behavior Modification.* Advance online publication. https://doi.org/10.1177/0145445518792251

Cross, R. M. (2005). Exploring attitudes: The case for Q methodology. *Health Education Research, 20*(2), 206–213. https://doi.org/10.1093/her/cyg121

Dahan, H., & Bedos, C. (2010). A typology of dental students according to their experience of stress: A qualitative study. *Journal of Dental Education, 74*(2), 95–103. https://doi.org/10.1002/j.0022-0337.2010.74.2.tb04858.x

DiCicco-Bloom, B., & Crabtree, B. F. (2006). The qualitative research interview. *Medical Education, 40*(4), 314–321. https://doi.org/10.1111/j.1365-2929.2006.02418.x

Eckshtain, D., & Weisz, J. R. (2019). Making sense of youth psychotherapy dropout from depression treatment [Editorial]. *Journal of the American Academy of Child & Adolescent Psychiatry, 58*(10), 945–947. https://doi.org/10.1016/j.jaac.2019.04.008

Edgley, A., Stickley, T., Timmons, S., & Meal, A. (2016). Critical realist review: Exploring the real, beyond the empirical. *Journal of Further and Higher Education, 40*(3), 316–330. https://doi.org/10.1080/0309877X.2014.953458

Eisenstadt, M. (2020). *How can qualitative investigations into adolescent experiences of stressors, risk factors and protective factors further our understanding of mental well-being and the prevention of psychopathology during adolescence in England?* [Unpublished doctoral dissertation]. University College London.

Eisenstadt, M., Stapley, E., & Deighton, J. (2020). *Learning from young people in HeadStart: A study of young people's reported protective factors in relation to risk factors and wellbeing.* Evidence Based Practice Unit.

Elliott, R., Fischer, C. T., & Rennie, D. L. (1999). Evolving guidelines for publication of qualitative research studies in psychology and related fields. *British Journal of Clinical Psychology, 38*(3), 215–229. https://doi.org/10.1348/014466599162782

Flurey, C. A., Hewlett, S., Rodham, K., White, A., Noddings, R., & Kirwan, J. R. (2016). Identifying different typologies of experiences and coping strategies in men with rheumatoid arthritis: A Q-methodology study. *BMJ Open, 6*(10), e012051. https://doi.org/10.1136/bmjopen-2016-012051

Frommer, J., Langenbach, M., & Streeck, U. (2004). Qualitative psychotherapy research in German-speaking countries. *Psychotherapy Research, 14*(1), 57–75. https://doi.org/10.1093/ptr/kph004

Gerhardt, U. (1994). The use of Weberian ideal-type methodology in qualitative data interpretation: An outline for ideal-type analysis. *Bulletin de Methodologie Sociologique, 45*(1), 74–126. https://doi.org/10.1177/075910639404500105

Gerring, J. (2004). What is a case study and what is it good for? *The American Political Science Review, 98*(2), 341–354. https://doi.org/10.1017/S0003055404001182

Gisslevik, E., Wernersson, I., & Larsson, C. (2019). Pupils' participation in and response to sustainable food education in Swedish home and consumer studies: A case-study. *Scandinavian Journal of Educational Research, 63*(4), 585–604. https://doi.org/10.1080/00313831.2017.1415965

Glaser, B. G. (1992). *Basics of grounded theory analysis.* Sociological Press.

Goodyer, I. M., Reynolds, S., Barrett, B., Byford, S., Dubicka, B., Hill, J., Holland, F., Kelvin, R., Midgley, N., Roberts, C., Senior, R., Target, M., Widmer, B., Wilkinson, P., & Fonagy, P. (2017). Cognitive behavioural therapy and short-term psychoanalytical psychotherapy versus a brief psychosocial intervention in adolescents with unipolar major depressive disorder (IMPACT): A multicentre, pragmatic, observer-blind, randomised controlled superiority trial. *The Lancet Psychiatry, 4*(2), 109–119. https://doi.org/10.1016/S2215-0366(16)30378-9

Goodyer, I. M., Tsancheva, S., Byford, S., Dubicka, B., Hill, J., Kelvin, R., Reynolds, S., Roberts, C., Senior, R., Suckling, J., Wilkinson, P., Target, M., & Fonagy, P. (2011). Improving mood with psychoanalytic and cognitive therapies (IMPACT): A pragmatic effectiveness superiority trial to investigate whether specialised psychological treatment reduces the risk for relapse in adolescents with moderate to severe unipolar depression: Study protocol for a randomised controlled trial. *Trials, 12*(1), 175. https://doi.org/10.1186/1745-6215-12-175

Gower, J. C. (1971). A general coefficient of similarity and some of its properties. *Biometrics, 27*(4), 857–871. https://doi.org/10.2307/2528823

Griffiths, F. E., Lindenmeyer, A., Borkan, J., Donner Banzhoff, N., Lamb, S., Parchman, M., & Sturt, J. (2014). Case typologies, chronic illness and primary health care. *Journal of Evaluation in Clinical Practice, 20*(4), 513–521. https://doi.org/10.1111/jep.12070

Grytnes, R. (2011). Making the right choice! Inquiries into the reasoning behind young people's decisions about education. *Young, 19*(3), 333–351. https://doi.org/10.1177/110330881101900305

Henry, D. B., Tolan, P. H., & Gorman-Smith, D. (2005). Cluster analysis in family psychology research. *Journal of Family Psychology, 19*(1), 121–132. https://doi.org/10.1037/0893-3200.19.1.121

Hill, C. E., Knox, S., Thompson, B. J., Williams, E. N., Hess, S. A., & Ladany, N. (2005). Consensual Qualitative Research: An update. *Journal of Counseling Psychology, 52*(2), 196–205. https://doi.org/10.1037/0022-0167.52.2.196

Jacobsen, T., & Hofmann, V. (1997). Children's attachment representations: Longitudinal relations to school behavior and academic competency in middle childhood and adolescence. *Developmental Psychology, 33*(4), 703–710. https://doi.org/10.1037/0012-1649.33.4.703

Jungbauer, J., Wittmund, B., Dietrich, S., & Angermeyer, M. C. (2003). Subjective burden over 12 months in parents of patients with schizophrenia. *Archives of Psychiatric Nursing, 17*(3), 126–134. https://doi.org/10.1016/S0883-9417(03)00056-6

Kallio, H., Pietilä, A. M., Johnson, M., & Kangasniemi, M. (2016). Systematic methodological review: Developing a framework for a qualitative semi-structured interview guide. *Journal of Advanced Nursing, 72*, 2954–2965. https://doi.org/10.1111/jan.13031

Kettunen, E., Kemppainen, T., Lievonen, M., Makkonen, M., Frank, L., & Kari, T. (2018, September 28–30). *Ideal types of online shoppers: A qualitative analysis of online shopping behavior* [Paper presentation]. Mediterranean Conference on Information Systems, Corfu, Greece.

King, G., Keohane, R. O., & Verba, S. (1994). *Designing social inquiry: Scientific inference in qualitative research.* Princeton University Press. https://doi.org/10.1515/9781400821211

Kluge, S. (2000). Empirically grounded construction of types and typologies in qualitative social research. *Forum: Qualitative Social Research, 1*(1), 14. https://www.qualitative-research.net/index.php/fqs/article/view/1124/2499

Koenigsmann, M., Koehler, K., Regner, A., Franke, A., & Frommer, J. (2006). Facing mortality: A qualitative in-depth interview study on illness perception, lay theories and coping strategies of adult patients with acute leukemia

1 week after diagnosis. *Leukemia Research, 30*(9), 1127–1134. https://doi.org/10.1016/j.leukres.2005.12.016

Kuckartz, U. (1991). Ideal types or empirical types: The case of Max Weber's empirical research. *Bulletin de Methodologie Sociologique, 32*(1), 44–53. https://doi.org/10.1177/075910639103200103

Kühnlein, I. (1999). Psychotherapy as a process of transformation: Analysis of posttherapeutic autobiographic narrations. *Psychotherapy Research, 9*(3), 274–287.

Kvist, J. (2007). Fuzzy set ideal type analysis. *Journal of Business Research, 60*(5), 474–481. https://doi.org/10.1016/j.jbusres.2007.01.005

Landis, J. R., & Koch, G. G. (1977). The measurement of observer agreement for categorical data. *Biometrics, 33*(1), 159–174. https://doi.org/10.2307/2529310

Langenbach, M., Kuhn-Régnier, F., & Geissler, H. J. (2002). Patients' subjective reconstruction of meaning after heart transplantation. *Transplantation Proceedings, 34*(6), 2183–2184. https://doi.org/10.1016/S0041-1345(02)03196-2

Legewie, N. (2013). An introduction to applied data analysis with qualitative comparative analysis. *Forum: Qualitative Social Research, 7*(4). https://www.qualitative-research.net/index.php/fqs/article/view/1961

Levitt, H. M., Bamberg, M., Creswell, J. W., Frost, D. M., Josselson, R., & Suárez-Orozco, C. (2018). Journal article reporting standards for qualitative primary, qualitative meta-analytic, and mixed methods research in psychology: The APA Publications and Communications Board task force report. *American Psychologist, 73*(1), 26–46. https://doi.org/10.1037/amp0000151

Lewin, S., Glenton, C., & Oxman, A. D. (2009). Use of qualitative methods alongside randomised controlled trials of complex healthcare interventions: Methodological study. *BMJ, 339*, b3496. https://doi.org/10.1136/bmj.b3496

Lindner, R. (2006). Suicidality in men in psychodynamic psychotherapy. *Psychoanalytic Psychotherapy, 20*(3), 197–217. https://doi.org/10.1080/02668730600868948

Lindner, R., & Briggs, S. (2010). Forming ideal types by understanding: The psychoanalytic treatment of suicidal men. *Forum: Qualitative Social Research, 11*(2), 12. https://www.qualitative-research.net/index.php/fqs/article/view/1278/2977

Lindner, R., Fiedler, G., Altenhofer, A., Gotze, P., & Happach, C. (2006). Psychodynamic ideal types of elderly suicidal persons based on counter transference. *Journal of Social Work Practice, 20*, 347–365. https://doi.org/10.1080/02650530600932011

Madill, A., Jordan, A., & Shirley, C. (2000). Objectivity and reliability in qualitative analysis: Realist, contextualist and radical constructionist epistemologies. *British Journal of Psychology, 91*(1), 1–20. https://doi.org/10.1348/000712600161646

Main, M., & Solomon, J. (1990). Procedures for identifying disorganized/disoriented infants during the Ainsworth Strange Situation. In M. Greenberg, D. Cicchetti, & M. Cummings (Eds.), *Attachment in the preschool years* (pp. 121–160). University of Chicago Press.

Malterud, K. (2001). Qualitative research: Standards, challenges, and guidelines. *The Lancet, 358*(9280), 483–488. https://doi.org/10.1016/S0140-6736(01)05627-6

Mandara, J. (2003). The typological approach in child and family psychology: A review of theory, methods, and research. *Clinical Child and Family Psychology Review, 6*, 129–146. https://doi.org/10.1023/A:1023734627624

Maxwell, J. A. (2010). *A realist approach for qualitative research.* SAGE.

McIntosh, D. (1977). The objective bases of Max Weber's ideal types. *History and Theory, 16*(3), 265–279. https://doi.org/10.2307/2504833

McLeod, J. (2011). *Qualitative research in counselling and psychotherapy* (2nd ed.). SAGE.

Mehrinejad, S. A., Rajabimoghadam, S., & Tarsafi, M. (2015). The relationship between parenting styles and creativity and the predictability of creativity by parenting styles. *Procedia—Social and Behavioral Sciences, 205*(May), 56–60. https://doi.org/10.1016/j.sbspro.2015.09.014

Midgley, N., Ansaldo, F., Parkinson, S., Holmes, J., Stapley, E., & Target, M. (2011). *Experience of Therapy Interview (Young Person, Parent and Therapist Versions).* Anna Freud Centre.

Midgley, N., Ansaldo, F., & Target, M. (2014). The meaningful assessment of therapy outcomes: Incorporating a qualitative study into a randomized controlled trial evaluating the treatment of adolescent depression. *Psychotherapy, 51*(1), 128–137. https://doi.org/10.1037/a0034179

Midgley, N., Holmes, J., Parkinson, S., Stapley, E., Eatough, V., & Target, M. (2016). "Just like talking to someone about like shit in your life and stuff, and they help you": Hopes and expectations for therapy among depressed adolescents. *Psychotherapy Research, 26*(1), 11–21. https://doi.org/10.1080/10503307.2014.973922

Milford, C., Kriel, Y., Njau, I., Nkole, T., Gichangi, P., Cordero, J. P., Smit, J. A., Steyn, P. S., & The UPTAKE Project Research Team. (2017). Teamwork in qualitative research: Descriptions of a multicountry team approach. *International Journal of Qualitative Methods, 16*(1). https://doi.org/10.1177/1609406917727189

O'Connor, C., & Joffe, H. (2020). Intercoder reliability in qualitative research: Debates and practical guidelines. *International Journal of Qualitative Methods, 19.* https://doi.org/10.1177/1609406919899220

O'Keeffe, S., Martin, P., Goodyer, I., Kelvin, R., Dubicka, B., IMPACT Consortium, & Midgley, N. (2019). Prognostic implications for adolescents with depression who drop out of psychological treatment during a randomized controlled trial. *Journal of the American Academy of Child & Adolescent Psychiatry, 58*(10), 983–992. https://doi.org/10.1016/j.jaac.2018.11.019

O'Keeffe, S., Martin, P., Target, M., & Midgley, N. (2019, February). 'I just stopped going': A mixed methods investigation into types of therapy dropout in adolescents with depression. *Frontiers in Psychology, 10,* 75. https://doi.org/10.3389/fpsyg.2019.00075

Ormhaug, S. M., & Jensen, T. K. (2018). Investigating treatment characteristics and first-session relationship variables as predictors of dropout in the treatment of traumatized youth. *Psychotherapy Research, 28*(2), 235–249. https://doi.org/10.1080/10503307.2016.1189617

Ortlipp, M. (2008). Keeping and using reflective journals in the qualitative research process. *Qualitative Report, 13*(4), 695–705. https://nsuworks.nova.edu/tqr/vol13/iss4/8

Philips, B., Wennberg, P., & Werbart, A. (2007). Ideas of cure as a predictor of premature termination, early alliance and outcome in psychoanalytic psychotherapy. *Psychology and Psychotherapy, 80*(2), 229–245. https://doi.org/10.1348/147608306X128266

Philips, B., Werbart, A., Wennberg, P., & Schubert, J. (2007). Young adults' ideas of cure prior to psychoanalytic psychotherapy. *Journal of Clinical Psychology, 63*(3), 213–232. https://doi.org/10.1002/jclp.20342

Psathas, G. (2005). The ideal type in Weber and Schutz. *Explorations of the Life-World,* 144–169. https://doi.org/10.1007/1-4020-3220-X_7

Rihoux, B. (2003). Bridging the gap between the qualitative and quantitative worlds? A retrospective and prospective view on qualitative comparative analysis. *Field Methods, 15*(4), 351–365. https://doi.org/10.1177/1525822X03257690

Riley, T., & Hawe, P. (2009). A typology of practice narratives during the implementation of a preventive, community intervention trial. *Implementation Science, 4*(1), 80. https://doi.org/10.1186/1748-5908-4-80

Ritchie, J., & Spencer, L. (1994). Qualitative data analysis for applied policy research. In A. Bryman & R. G. Burgess (Eds.), *Analyzing qualitative data* (pp. 173–194). Routledge. https://doi.org/10.4324/9780203413081_chapter_9

Robinson, O. C., & Smith, J. A. (2010). Investigating the form and dynamics of crisis episodes in early adulthood: The application of a composite qualitative method. *Qualitative Research in Psychology, 7*(2), 170–191. https://doi.org/10.1080/14780880802699084

Rodriguez-Morales, L. (2017). In your own skin: The experience of early recovery from alcohol-use disorder in 12-step fellowships. *Alcoholism Treatment Quarterly, 35*(4), 372–394. https://doi.org/10.1080/07347324.2017.1355204

Roulston, K., & Shelton, S. A. (2015). Reconceptualizing bias in teaching qualitative research methods. *Qualitative Inquiry, 21*(4), 332–342. https://doi.org/10.1177/1077800414563803

Salomonsson, B., & Sandell, R. (2011). A randomized controlled trial of mother–infant psychoanalytic treatment: II. Predictive and moderating influences of qualitative patient factors. *Infant Mental Health Journal, 32*(3), 377–404. https://doi.org/10.1002/imhj.20302

Sanjari, M., Bahramnezhad, F., Fomani, F. K., Sho-Ghi, M., & Cheraghi, M. A. (2014). Ethical challenges of researchers in qualitative studies: The necessity to develop a specific guideline. *Journal of Medical Ethics and History of Medicine, 7*(14), 1–6.

Schutz, A. (1967). *The phenomenology of the social world*. Northwestern University Press.

Sharp, N. L., Bye, R. A., & Cusick, A. (2018). Narrative analysis. In P. Liamputtong (Ed.), *Handbook of research methods in health social sciences* (pp. 1–21). Springer. https://doi.org/10.1007/978-981-10-2779-6_106-1

Shenton, A. K. (2004). Strategies for ensuring trustworthiness in qualitative research projects. *Education for Information, 22*(2), 63–75. https://doi.org/10.3233/EFI-2004-22201

Sidnell, J., & Stivers, T. (Eds.). (2013). *The handbook of conversation analysis*. Wiley. https://doi.org/10.1016/j.bar.2008.07.006

Simons, L. G., & Conger, R. D. (2007). Linking mother–father differences in parenting styles and adolescent outcomes. *Journal of Family Issues, 28*(2), 212–241. https://doi.org/10.1177/0192513X06294593

Smith, J. A. (2015). *Qualitative psychology: A practical guide to research methods*. SAGE.

Smith, J. A., Flowers, P., & Larkin, M. (2009). *Interpretative phenomenological analysis: Theory, method and research*. SAGE.

Stapley, E. (2016). *Journey through the shadows: The experience of being the parent of an adolescent diagnosed with depression* [Unpublished doctoral dissertation]. University College London.

Stapley, E., Eisenstadt, M., Demkowicz, O., Stock, S., & Deighton, J. (2020). *Learning from young people in HeadStart: A study of change over time in young people's experiences of difficulties and support*. Evidence Based Practice Unit.

Stapley, E., Target, M., & Midgley, N. (2017). The journey through and beyond mental health services in the United Kingdom: A typology of parents' ways of managing the crisis of their teenage child's depression. *Journal of Clinical Psychology, 73*(10), 1429–1441. https://doi.org/10.1002/jclp.22446

Stoecker, R. (2003). Community-based research: From practice to theory and back again. *Michigan Journal of Community Service Learning, 9*, 35.

Strauss, A., & Corbin, J. (1998). *Basics of qualitative research techniques: Techniques and procedures for developing grounded theory*. SAGE.

Stuhr, U., & Wachholz, S. (2001). In search for a psychoanalytic research strategy: The concept of ideal types. *Psychologische Beiträge, 43*(3).

Swedberg, R. (2018). How to use Max Weber's ideal type in sociological analysis. *Journal of Classical Sociology, 18*(3), 181–196. https://doi.org/10.1177/1468795X17743643

Towers, E., & Maguire, M. (2017). Leaving or staying in teaching: A 'vignette' of an experienced urban teacher 'leaver' of a London primary school. *Teachers and Teaching: Theory and Practice, 23*(8), 946–960. https://doi.org/10.1080/13540602.2017.1358703

Tufford, L., & Newman, P. (2012). Bracketing in qualitative research. *Qualitative Social Work: Research and Practice, 11*(1), 80–96. https://doi.org/10.1177/1473325010368316

Vachon, M., Fillion, L., & Achille, M. (2012). Death confrontation, spiritual–existential experience and caring attitudes in palliative care nurses: An interpretative phenomenological analysis. *Qualitative Research in Psychology, 9*(2), 151–172. https://doi.org/10.1080/14780881003663424

Valkonen, J., Hanninen, V., & Lindfors, O. (2011). Outcomes of psychotherapy from the perspective of the users. *Psychotherapy Research, 21*(2), 227–240. https://doi.org/10.1080/10503307.2010.548346

Vandoninck, S., & d'Haenens, L. (2015). Children's online coping strategies: Rethinking coping typologies in a risk-specific approach. *Journal of Adolescence, 45,* 225–236. https://doi.org/10.1016/j.adolescence.2015.10.007

Vogl, S., Zartler, U., Schmidt, E. M., & Rieder, I. (2018). Developing an analytical framework for multiple perspective, qualitative longitudinal interviews (MPQLI). *International Journal of Social Research Methodology, 21*(2), 177–190. https://doi.org/10.1080/13645579.2017.1345149

Vollrath, M., & Torgersen, S. (2002). Who takes health risks? A probe into eight personality types. *Personality and Individual Differences, 32*(7), 1185–1197. https://doi.org/10.1016/S0191-8869(01)00080-0

Wachholz, S., & Stuhr, U. (1999). The concept of ideal types in psychoanalytic follow-up research. *Psychotherapy Research, 9*(3), 327–341.

Walker, D., & Myrick, F. (2006). Grounded theory: An exploration of process and procedure. *Qualitative Health Research, 16,* 547–559. https://doi.org/10.1177/1049732305285972

Warnick, E. M., Gonzalez, A., Weersing, V. R., Scahill, L., & Woolston, J. (2012). Defining dropout from youth psychotherapy: How definitions shape the prevalence and predictors of attrition. *Child and Adolescent Mental Health, 17*(2), 76–85. https://doi.org/10.1111/j.1475-3588.2011.00606.x

Weber, M. (1904). *Methodology of social sciences*. Routledge.

Werbart, A., Brusell, L., Iggedal, R., Lavfors, K., & Widholm, A. (2016). Changes in self-representations following psychoanalytic psychotherapy for young adults: A comparative typology. *Journal of the American Psychoanalytic Association, 64*(5), 917–958. https://doi.org/10.1177/0003065116676765

Werbart, A., Grünbaum, C., Jonasson, B., Kempe, H., Kusz, M., Linde, S., O'Nils, K. L., Sjövall, P., Svenson, M., Theve, C., Ulin, L., & Öhlin, A. (2011). Changes in the representations of mother and father among young adults in psychoanalytic psychotherapy. *Psychoanalytic Psychology, 28*(1), 95–116. https://doi.org/10.1037/a0022344

Williams, M. (2002). Generalization in interpretive research. In T. May (Ed.), *Qualitative research in action* (pp. 125–143). SAGE. https://doi.org/10.4135/9781849209656

Willig, C. (2012). Perspectives on the epistemological bases for qualitative research. In H. Cooper, P. M. Camic, D. L. Long, A. T. Panter, D. Rindskopf, & K. J. Sher (Eds.), *APA handbook of research methods in psychology: Vol 1. Foundations, planning, measures, and psychometrics* (pp. 5–21). American Psychological Association. https://doi.org/10.1037/13619-002

Willig, C. (2016). Constructivism and "the real world": Can they co-exist? *QMiP Bulletin, 21*, 33–37.

Yardley, L. (2000). Dilemmas in qualitative health research. *Psychology & Health, 15*(2), 215–228. https://doi.org/10.1080/08870440008400302

Index

A

Ainsworth, M. D., 37
American Psychological Association
    (APA), 49
Armstrong, D., 24
Attachment researchers, 13, 37
Audio recording, consent for, 21

B

Becoming familiarized with data set (step 1)
    about, 28, 29
    example, 67
    research team for, 22
Behavior, human, 12–13, 80
Bell, S. M., 13, 37
Biases, 81
Borderline cases, 36–37, 70
Braun, V., 29, 59
Briggs, S., 24, 27

C

Case reconstructions, writing. *See* Writing
    case reconstructions (step 2)
Case study research approach, limitations
    of, 10–11
Charmaz, K., 23
Checking credibility (step 6)
    about, 28, 43–45
    example, 72–76
Child and adolescent mental health
    services (CAMHS), 30–32, 34, 39, 47
Clarke, V., 29, 59
Cluster analysis, 4

Cohen's kappa, 44
Confidentiality, 21, 52, 64–65
Consent, informed, 21, 64
Consent form, 21
Constructing ideal types (step 3)
    about, 28, 34–39
    example, 69–70
Constructivist epistemological perspective,
    8–9
    of typology construction, 81
    and typology credibility, 24
Conversation analysis, 18
Creativity, 55
Credibility checks
    about, 28, 43–45
    example, 72–76
    and research subjectivity, 23–24
    and sample size, 18
"Critical friends," 23
Critical realism, 8, 9, 24
Cross-case research approach,
    limitations of, 10

D

Data
    analysis of. *See* Data analysis
    collecting. *See* Data collection
    in constructivist epistemological
        perspective, 8–9
    familiarization with set of (step 1),
        22, 28, 29, 67
    longitudinal qualitative, 56–57
    multiple types of, 57–58

naturally occurring, 20
qualitative. *See* Qualitative data
Data analysis. *See also* Methodology
   deciding method for (example), 65–66
   example, 67–77
   writing about, in methodology section,
     51
Data collection, 18–21
   example, 63–64
   using multiple types of data, 57–58
   writing about, in methodology section,
     50–51
Description of groups of participants, 11–12
Discussion section, 53

E

Eisenstadt, Mia, 31, 52–53
Epistemological position, defining, 66–67
Epistemology, 7–9
Ethical considerations
   example, 64–65
   in qualitative data collection, 20–21
   writing about, in methodology section,
     51
Ethnographic research, 6
Experience of Therapy Interview, 63

F

Flexibility, 80
Forming ideal-type descriptions (step 5)
   about, 28, 41–43
   example, 75
Framework analysis, 5

G

Gerhardt, Uta, 6–8, 14, 27, 29, 39, 79
Gisslevik, E., 20, 59
Gower distance, 73
Griffiths, F. E., 45
Grounded theory
   and constructing ideal types, 35
   constructivist epistemological
     perspective of, 9
   and ideal-type analysis development, 6
   in qualitative research, 10
Groups of participants
   credibility checks through discussion
     with, 45
   description of, 11–12

forming, 80
individuals compared with, 12
qualitative data from multiple, 57

H

Heterogeneity, of sample, 17
Hofmann, V., 13
"How" research questions, 16
Human behavior, 12–13, 80
Human thought, 12–13

I

Ideal, as term, 6
Ideal type(s)
   constructing (step 3), 28, 34–39, 69–70
   in discussion section, 53
   forming descriptions of (step 5), 28,
     41–43, 75
   as hypothesis of human thought and
     behavior, 12–13
Ideal-type analysis
   benefits and advantages of, 80
   epistemology and, 7–9
   key features of, 11–14
   limitations of, 80–82
   with longitudinal qualitative data, 56–57
   methodology of. *See* Methodology
   with multiple types of data, 57–58
   origins of, 5–7
   with qualitative data from multiple
     groups of participants, 57
   as second stage of qualitative data
     analysis, 58–59
   and typologies in psychology, 4–5
   uses of, 15–17
Identifying optimal cases (step 4)
   about, 28, 39–41
   example, 75
IMPACT-My Experience (IMPACT-ME)
   study, 62–63
IMPACT (Improving Mood With
   Psychoanalytic and Cognitive
   Therapies) trial, 62–63
In-depth interviews, for data collection, 19
Individuals, groups compared with, 12
Informed consent, 21, 64
Interpretative phenomenological analysis
   (IPA)
   about, 18
   data collection for, 18

example, 65
performing ideal-type analysis after, 58
Interviews
example, 63–64
in-depth, for data collection, 19
semistructured, 19–20, 50–51
writing case reconstructions with data
from, 29–30, 32–33
Introduction, 49–50
IPA. *See* Interpretative phenomenological
analysis

J

Jacobsen, T., 13
Joffe, H., 24
Jungbauer, J., 36

K

Kettunen, E., 58

L

Levitt, H. M., 49, 53
Lindner, R., 13, 24, 27
Longitudinal qualitative data, 56–57

M

Making comparisons (step 7)
about, 28, 45–47
example, 76–77
Manuscript, 49–53
discussion section, 53
example, 77–78
introduction, 49–50
methodology section, 50–51
results section, 51–53
Martin, P., 34, 36, 44, 57, 68–69, 71, 74
Methodology, 27–47. *See also* Data analysis
about, 79–80
becoming familiarized with data set
(step 1), 29
checking credibility (step 6), 43–45
constructing ideal types (step 3), 34–39
development of, 7
example, 65–77
forming ideal-type descriptions (step 5),
41–43
identifying optimal cases (step 4),
39–41

making comparisons (step 7), 45–47
and research teams, 22
variations of, 55–59
writing case reconstructions (step 2),
29–34
Methodology section, 50–51
Midgley, N., 19, 34, 36, 44, 57, 61, 68–69,
71, 74
Multiple types of data, 57–58

N

Narrative analysis, 5
Naturally occurring data, 20
Number of cases, 17

O

Observations, data collection through, 20
O'Connor, C., 24
O'Keeffe, S., 34, 36, 44, 57, 61, 68–69,
71, 74. *See also* Treatment dropout
study
Optimal cases, 12, 28, 39–41, 75

P

Parenting styles, typologies of, 4
Participants
groups of. *See* Groups of participants
writing about, in methodology section,
50
Philips, B., 13, 27
Predictive validity, 13
Prototypes. *See* Optimal cases
Pseudonyms, 52, 77
Psychology
case studies used in, 11
typologies in, 4–5
Psychotherapy researchers, 16–17
Purposive sampling, 18

Q

Q-methodology, 4
Qualitative cluster analysis, 13–14
Qualitative comparative analysis, 4
Qualitative data
ethical considerations in collecting,
20–21
ideal-type analysis of, 9–11
from multiple groups of participants, 57

R

Randomized controlled trial (RCT), 62
Realism, 8
Realism, critical, 8, 9, 24
Recordings, consent for, 21
Reflective diary, 23
Reflexivity, 9, 81
Researcher subjectivity, 7–8, 23–25
Research–participant alliance, 21
Research questions
    and constructing ideal types, 34
    for designing study, 15–16, 25
    developing (example), 61–62
Research team
    for analysis to construct ideal types, 37
    and case sorting, 36
    need for and role of, 21–22
Respondent-driven sampling, 18
Results section, 51–53

S

Salomonsson, B., 58
Samples, 17–18, 63
Sandell, R., 58
Schizophrenia, 36
Semistructured interviews, 19–20, 50–51
Stapley, E., 17, 34, 37–40, 42, 44, 46–47, 56, 81
Statistical cluster analysis, 13–14
Study design, 15–26
    data collection, 18–21
    and researcher subjectivity, 23–25
    research team, 21–22
    sample size, 17–18
Stuhr, U., 27–28, 33
Subjectivity, researcher, 7–8, 23–25

T

Target, M., 34, 36, 44, 57, 68–69, 71, 74
Team. *See* Research team
Thematic analysis, 10, 59, 65
Therapy sessions, data collection from, 20
Thought, human, 12–13
Transcripts
    and becoming familiarized with
        data set, 29
    in results section, 52
    using, for credibility checks, 43

using, for data collection, 18
writing case reconstruction using, 29
Treatment dropout study, 61–78. *See also*
    O'Keeffe, S.
    context for, 62–63
    data collection, 63–64
    deciding how to analyze data in, 65–66
    defining epistemological position in,
        66–67
    developing research question, 61–62
    ethical considerations, 64–65
    methodology, 67–77
    sample, 63
    writing manuscript for, 77–78
Typology
    aims of developing, 15
    checking credibility of, 18, 23–24,
        43–45
    constructing initial (example), 70–71
    defining, 4–5
    and description of groups of
        participants, 11–12
    as hypothesis of human thought and
        behavior, 12–13
    importance of ideal-type analysis for
        developing, 80
    limitations of constructing, 81

V

Vachon, M., 9
Validity, predictive, 13
Video recording, consent for, 21

W

Wachholz, S., 27–28, 33
Weber, Max, 5–7, 14, 79
Wennberg, P., 13
Werbart, A., 13, 17–18, 27–28, 38–39, 43,
    56, 81
"What" research questions, 16
"Why" research questions, 16
Willig, C., 9
Within case research approaches,
    limitations of, 10–11
Writing case reconstructions (step 2)
    about, 29–30, 32–33
    example, 67–69
    examples, 31–34
    organization of content for, 34
    research teams for, 22

About the Authors

Emily Stapley, PhD, is a research fellow in the Evidence Based Practice Unit (EBPU), Anna Freud National Centre for Children and Families and University College London (UCL). Dr. Stapley's research interests center on investigating young people's and families' experiences of mental health problems, coping, and receiving support. Dr. Stapley has expertise in conducting qualitative and mixed-methods research. Her doctoral research at UCL examined the experiences of parents of adolescents diagnosed with and receiving therapy for depression in England. Dr. Stapley's current research within the EBPU qualitatively captures the experiences of children and adolescents in receipt of preventive interventions in school and community settings, which seek to promote positive mental health and well-being. Her research focuses on young people's perspectives on these interventions, as well as on the other coping strategies and sources of support that they report drawing on to manage their mental health.

Sally O'Keeffe, PhD, is a research fellow in the School of Health Sciences at City, University of London. She has worked on clinical trials investigating the effectiveness of psychological interventions, including treatments for depression and self-harm. Dr. O'Keeffe is particularly interested in the use of mixed methods to explore how interventions work and what works for whom. She completed her PhD at University College London and the Anna Freud National Centre for Children and Families. Her PhD was a mixed-methods investigation into psychotherapy dropout in adolescents with a diagnosis of depression. In 2018, she was awarded the Counselling Research Award for her PhD work from the Counselling and Psychotherapy Central Awarding Body (CPCAB). Currently, Dr. O'Keeffe is working on a research program to develop a brief psychological intervention for people presenting to emergency departments having self-harmed.

Nick Midgley, PhD, is a professor of psychological therapies with children and young people at University College London and the Anna Freud National Centre for Children and Families, where he is codirector of the Child Attachment and Psychological Therapies Research Unit. He has written and edited many articles and books, including *Essential Research Findings in Child and Adolescent Counselling and Psychotherapy* (SAGE, 2017); *Mentalization-Based Treatment for Children: A Time-Limited Approach* (American Psychological Association, 2017); and *So Young, So Sad, So Listen: A Parent's Guide to Depression in Children and Young People* (Cambridge University Press, 2020). Dr. Midgley draws on qualitative and mixed-methods approaches in his research, which has included studies on the treatment of adolescent depression and the evaluation of interventions to support children in foster care. He was the recipient of the Early Career Achievement Award from the Society for Psychotherapy Research in 2013 and the British Association of Counselling and Psychotherapy's Outstanding Research Award in 2019.

About the Series Editors

Clara E. Hill, PhD, earned her doctorate at Southern Illinois University in 1974. She started her career in 1974 as an assistant professor in the Department of Psychology, University of Maryland, College Park, and is currently there as a professor.

She is the president-elect of the Society for the Advancement of Psychotherapy, and has been the president of the Society for Psychotherapy Research, the editor of the *Journal of Counseling Psychology*, and the editor of *Psychotherapy Research*.

Dr. Hill was awarded the Leona Tyler Award for Lifetime Achievement in Counseling Psychology from Division 17 (Society of Counseling Psychology) and the Distinguished Psychologist Award from Division 29 (Society for the Advancement of Psychotherapy) of the American Psychological Association, the Distinguished Research Career Award from the Society for Psychotherapy Research, and the Outstanding Lifetime Achievement Award from the Section on Counseling and Psychotherapy Process and Outcome Research of the Society for Counseling Psychology. Her major research interests are helping skills, psychotherapy process and outcome, training therapists, dream work, and qualitative research.

She has published more than 250 journal articles, 80 chapters in books, and 17 books (including *Therapist Techniques and Client Outcomes: Eight Cases of Brief Psychotherapy*; *Helping Skills: Facilitating Exploration, Insight, and Action*; and *Dream Work in Therapy: Facilitating Exploration, Insight, and Action*).

Sarah Knox, PhD, joined the faculty of Marquette University in 1999 and is a professor in the Department of Counselor Education and Counseling Psychology in the College of Education. She earned her doctorate at the

University of Maryland and completed her predoctoral internship at The Ohio State University.

Dr. Knox's research has been published in a number of journals, including *The Counseling Psychologist*, *Counselling Psychology Quarterly*, *Journal of Counseling Psychology*, *Psychotherapy*, *Psychotherapy Research*, and *Training and Education in Professional Psychology*. Her publications focus on the psychotherapy process and relationship, supervision and training, and qualitative research. She has presented her research both nationally and internationally and has provided workshops on consensual qualitative research at both U.S. and international venues.

She currently serves as coeditor-in-chief of *Counselling Psychology Quarterly* and is also on the publication board of Division 29 (Society for the Advancement of Psychotherapy) of the American Psychological Association. Dr. Knox is a fellow of Division 17 (Society of Counseling Psychology) and Division 29 (Society for the Advancement of Psychotherapy) of the American Psychological Association.